Navigating a Career in Technical Entertainment

Navigating a Career in Technical Entertainment: Your Creative Career Guidebook explores tools, strategies, and motivational advice from a wide range of industry professionals for navigating an artistic career in design and technology in entertainment.

This book is designed to accompany readers every step of the way in their career journey – from landing their first job after school through mid-career pivots and switching industries. It is organized into four parts: Finding Your Career Path; Tools and Strategies for Navigating Your Career Path; Curating a Creative Community as You Sustain Your Career; and Maintaining Flexibility and Finding Fulfillment in Your Career. Filled with motivational advice from mentors in the industry and creative worksheet exercises for personalized career planning, self-reflection, and goal setting, this book demystifies a complex industry, sharing crucial career-related information rarely covered in formal training programs. It explores a wide range of topics, including the types of jobs available in live entertainment and TV/film, education options, job searching, networking, career marketing materials, interviews, unions, financial empowerment, and refocusing on career shifts.

This guidebook is written for designers, technicians, stage managers, production managers, crew members, and creative technical artists in entertainment at all stages of their career. Covering a wide variety of entertainment from theater and television to commercials and theme parks, *Navigating a Career in Technical Entertainment* is a perfect companion for higher education or postsecondary educators and students exploring career and workforce readiness topics and can also be used by professionals actively working in the field.

This text also includes access to downloadable versions of the worksheets featured in the book, available at www.routledge.com/9780367510442.

Jessica Champagne Hansen is a costume designer and technician with experience in theater, dance, film, television, commercials, theme park, and corporate clients. She is Costume Faculty at East Los Angeles College in the Theater Arts Department and a member of United Scenic Artists Local 829.

Camille Schenkkan is the Deputy Managing Director at Center Theatre Group in Los Angeles and an Adjunct Faculty Member at Goucher College. She sits on the Board of Circle X Theatre Co, cochaired the National Emerging Leader Council through Americans for the Arts, and served as an issue expert for the Kennedy Center's Alliance for Arts Education Network.

Navigating a Career in Technical Entertainment
Your Creative Career Guidebook

Jessica Champagne Hansen and Camille Schenkkan

Routledge
Taylor & Francis Group

NEW YORK AND LONDON

Cover image: This cover has been designed using resources from Freepik.com and Macrovector.

First published 2023
by Routledge
605 Third Avenue, New York, NY 10158

and by Routledge
4 Park Square, Milton Park, Abingdon, Oxon, OX14 4RN

Routledge is an imprint of the Taylor & Francis Group, an informa business

© 2023 Taylor & Francis

The right of Jessica Champagne Hansen and Camille Schenkkan to be identified as authors of this work has been asserted in accordance with sections 77 and 78 of the Copyright, Designs and Patents Act 1988.

All rights reserved. No part of this book may be reprinted or reproduced or utilised in any form or by any electronic, mechanical, or other means, now known or hereafter invented, including photocopying and recording, or in any information storage or retrieval system, without permission in writing from the publishers.

Trademark notice: Product or corporate names may be trademarks or registered trademarks, and are used only for identification and explanation without intent to infringe.

Library of Congress Cataloging-in-Publication Data
A catalog record for this title has been requested

ISBN: 978-0-367-50303-1 (hbk)
ISBN: 978-0-367-51044-2 (pbk)
ISBN: 978-1-003-05222-7 (ebk)

DOI: 10.4324/9781003052227

Typeset in Optima
by Newgen Publishing UK

Access the Support Material: www.routledge.com/9780367510442

Dedication from Jessica:

This book is dedicated to the mentors that guide me as I navigate my own career journey.
Thank you to Rafael Jaen, for encouraging my creative spirit.
Thank you to Madeline Ann Kozlowski, for empowering the designer within.
Thank you to Michael Kasnetsis, for demonstrating unwavering dedication and tenacity.
Thank you to the ELAC Theater family, for always striving to be the best for our students and our community.

This book is also dedicated to the muses that inspire me to brave the unknown and follow my dreams.
Thank you to my husband, for relentless support and optimism.
Thank you to my children, for keeping me humble.
Thank you to my mother, for her acute perspective and always being right.
Thank you to my students, for allowing me to be a part of their story.
Thank you to my writing partner, Camille, for true collaboration and creative partnership! (We wrote a BOOK!)

Dedication from Camille:

To the Schenkkan Patrol: Zack, Ezra, Summer. I love you dearly.
To my mentors, JJ Lewis-Nichols, Tim Wright, Meghan Pressman, as well as the many other incredible teachers I've had—including my mama.
Thank you, Jessica, for bringing me into this project. It's been an honor to create alongside you! (We wrote a BOOK!)

Contents

List of Contributors ix

Introduction 1

Part I: Finding Your Career Path 3

   1 Introduction to Design and Technical Careers
      in Entertainment. 5

   2 Creative Industry Profiles 15

   3 Education, Degrees, and Training 33

Part II: Tools and Strategies for Navigating Your Career Path 53

   4 Job Searching and Networking 55

   5 Career Marketing Materials 73

   6 Interviews 103

**Part III: Curating a Creative Community as You Sustain
Your Career**. **121**

   7 Unions, Organizations, Groups, and Publications 123

   8 Creative Career Surviving and Thriving Skills 139

**Part IV: Maintaining Flexibility and Finding Fulfillment
in Your Career**. **167**

   9 Refocusing on Career Shifts and Wellness 169

  10 Self-Reflection and Goal Setting. 183

   Index. 197

Contributors

Ashley Bellet
Assistant Professor of Costume Design, Purdue University
Vice President for Commissions, USITT

Emily Bornt
Lighting Designer and Director

Sara Broadhead
Head Electrician, Segerstrom Hall at Segerstrom Center for the Arts

Brent Bruin
Pattern Maker and Fitter, IATSE Local 705 Motion Picture Costumers

Sean Cawelti
Creative Director, Immersive Video, Puppet and Mask Designer

Jane Childs
Director and Head of Faculty, Stagecraft Institute of Las Vegas

Courtney Clark
Arts Educator and Digital Marketer

Corinne Corillo
Sound Designer and Engineer

François-Pierre Couture
Professional Scenic, Lighting, and Projection Designer
Full Time Faculty, East Los Angeles College

Andy Crocker
Creative Consultant and Live Experience Designer

Rabbi Jessica Dell'Era
Rabbi

Ashley Diaz
Audio Engineer

Holly Poe Durbin
Professor, Head of Design
UC Irvine Claire Trevor School of the Arts
Costume Designer

Arpi Festekjian
Professor of Psychology, East Los Angeles College

Cristina Frias
Actor, Writer and Educator
Member of AEA & SAG-AFTRA

Johnathan Garza
Professional Staff House Committee on Natural Resources

Jennifer Goldstein
President, Radiance Lightworks, Inc.

Dianne K. Graebner
Costume Designer and University Lecturer

Chris Hansen
TV and Film Art Director and Production Designer

Howard Ho
Writer, Composer, and Youtuber

Meghan Ims
Costume Specialist and Project Manager

Aaron Jackson
Entertainment Designer
Founding Member and Creative Director of 2 Creative Entertainment

Serena Johnson
Career Clarity Coach
Founder, Get Me Out of This Job

Weston Keifer
Technical Manager of the Robinson Fine Arts Center at Plano Independent School District, Texas

Ann E. McMills
Head of Lighting Design, San Diego State University

Meagan Miller-McKeever
Set Decorator

J.M. Montecalvo
President and CEO, Spectrum401

Elena Muslar
Founder & Chief Empowerment Officer, Confide Creative

Merrianne Nedreberg
Prop Director, Center Theatre Group

Dr. Sergio Ramirez
Associate Dean, Admissions & Student Services at UCLA

Victoria Inez Rivera
Film and Television Costumer

Cheryl Rizzo
Managing Director, Boston Court Pasadena

Ashleigh Akilah Rucker
Writer, Director, Producer, and Program Director

Angela Scott
Education Director, Latino Theater Company Education Department

Josh Steadman
Art/Production Designer and Set Designer

Joel Veenstra
Actors' Equity Association Stage Manager
Production Manager, Producer, and Improviser

Diana Wyenn
Director

Introduction

Maybe you're a designer, or a technician, a stage manager, or a production manager. Maybe you think of yourself as an artist or creator, or as more of a facilitator, crew member, or manager.

Regardless, you're reading this book because you're interested in building a rewarding and sustainable career in the creative industries. These include theater and live entertainment, television and film, events, and even cruise ships and theme parks.

There are hundreds of distinct career pathways within these industries. Hoping to travel the world, moving from project to project? There are jobs for you. Prefer to stay in one place, with a steady paycheck and a consistent group of collaborators? Come on down.

Training for a career and working in that career are two very different things. Many traditional educational institutions, especially colleges and universities, have not focused entire courses or programs of study on workforce readiness topics such as how to find jobs or how to negotiate for fair payment. Instead, many focus mostly on studying craft and artistry with some supplementary information introducing workforce readiness concepts before completing the program. The goal of this book is to prepare you to find and enter into meaningful, rewarding work in your area of expertise.

While we recommend reading the book (and completing the exercises) in order, you can also flip to chapters that particularly interest you or feel especially relevant. Once you complete all the exercises, the last chapter will allow you to set strategic career goals, based on what you discover about your values, expertise, and interests.

We're glad you're here, both in this book and in the field. Welcome to your career in the creative industries!

DOI: 10.4324/9781003052227-1

Part I
Finding Your Career Path

1

Introduction to Design and Technical Careers in Entertainment

Career Guidebook Overview

This book is designed to accompany you in your career journey in a creative field. It is like a pocket mentor! Together, we will explore your career in four parts: Finding Your Career Path, Tools and Strategies for Navigating Your Career Path, Curating a Creative Community as You Sustain Your Career, and Maintaining Flexibility and Finding Fulfillment in Your Career.

In these parts, we will break down each phase of your career into smaller topics. How did we choose these topics? Well, they are all the things that we experienced on our career journey. Also, in talking with colleagues and students, these are also the topics that they wished were less of a mystery. Our goal is to bring this information to light and share it. When we are better informed as a community, we will all be stronger and better prepared together!

In Part I, Finding Your Career Path, we will explore creative industry profiles and look at different forms of education, degrees, and training. Part II is about job searching, networking, career marketing materials, and interviews. Part III focuses on sustaining your career with information about unions, organizations, groups, and publications. It also includes tips for both surviving and thriving in your creative career. Lastly, Part IV

DOI: 10.4324/9781003052227-3

is about refocusing on career shifts, self-reflection, and goal-setting, to ensure that you find fulfillment in your career.

The Reality of Careers in Entertainment

We all start our creative journey somewhere, with some sort of spark. At some point, each of us was captivated by the power of storytelling! That spark grows over time and develops into a dream of a creative job in entertainment. These creative fields are special because we were inspired by the generation before us, and our work will inspire the next generation. Someday, you will be the spark for someone else's creative journey.

The shift from dreaming about a creative career to the reality of actually working in the entertainment industry is a less magical process. At some point, we make the leap from studying and practicing our craft as a passion to trying to navigate how to make a sustainable living doing what we love. This is a hard shift and we often feel unprepared despite all our preparation and artistic skills.

We are told that it is hard. We are told that it does not pay well. We are told to have a back-up plan. We are told that we may not "make it." Many creative professionals tell similar stories about the messages given to them by well-meaning family, friends, and even teachers, about the viability of their chosen career path. It can be tempting to talk yourself out of pursuing these careers, just from the negative messages received from others.

Statements like this aren't particularly helpful, as they don't offer solutions, just challenges. It's our job – and the intention of this book – to take a solution-based approach to navigate the career you want and deserve, while also showing you how to cultivate a supportive creative community. The key is sharing information that others have learned along the way. Their tips and advice can be the solutions that you need to stay focused on your dreams.

In truth, some creative career pathways are tricky and can seem daunting as you first start out. Remember: it is brave to follow your dreams when there are so many uncertainties. Throughout this book, we will make a career map customized to YOU, to prepare for those uncertainties. With a personalized map, simple and practical steps, and knowledge about essential entertainment industry information, you will feel empowered to navigate your career journey with confidence. You've got this!

> **A Note on Mentors:** Although every creative journey is unique, there are breadcrumbs that have been left behind by those before us. Throughout this book, you'll find the voices of many professional mentors, sharing their stories, experiences, and advice. Their creative journeys began in many different ways and led them all to successful and sustainable careers in entertainment. We hope you enjoy their perspectives and that you consider mentoring the next generation as well!

Design and Technical Careers in Entertainment

This guidebook focuses on careers in entertainment. This includes, but is not limited to, theater, film, television, live entertainment, commercials, theme parks, cruise ships, corporate design, events, and more. The entertainment industry is ever-evolving and growing. It is a vibrant and exciting industry with so many opportunities for dynamic careers with your unique skills and experiences.

We will focus on the career details specific to designers and technicians, with additional information for managers, hybrid artists, and entrepreneurs. You don't have to choose one avenue, and together we will discover how to customize and curate your employment opportunities to best match your goals and skills. Also, designers and technicians can find work in adjacent industries based on their unique skillsets, such as video games, music industry, photography, journalism, events, publishing, education, museums, and more!

At the Heart of the Art: Why This Career?

No matter if you are a designer or a technician, you are an artist. Have you ever asked yourself, what kind of artist am I and why do I make art? Understanding why you chose a creative career and continue to choose it will help you stay motivated, inspired, and successful. In a challenging and competitive field, staying connected to your passion and joy is essential.

So, let's get started! We asked actress and "Citizen Artist" Cristina Frias to help us find our heart in the art. Together, we'll explore probing questions to help you find out what kind of artist you are and why you make art.

What Is Your Connection to Your Art and How Does Your Art Reflect Your Story?
The theater is Cristina's connection to the world and what connects her to both her home city and the world's stage. Because of her connection to the theater, she has always thought of herself as a "Global Artist" or "Citizen Artist." Cristina finds her heart in the art and shares, "Theater has ignited my imagination."

Cristina encourages you to find your story in your art and to

> find your connection. I have always been compelled by artistic projects that illuminate social issues and aim to transform the human experience. I am deeply connected to Theater for Social Justice and have worked closely with the Latinx Theater Community for most of my professional career.

What is your connection to the art and how does it reflect your story?

What Is Important to You in Your Life and in Your Art?
Think about what brings you joy and fulfillment in your creative work. For some people, it's the act of making art: being in rehearsal, working with your hands, or spending hours on a design. For others, it's the impact of the art: the way a play impacts an audience, or a movie can change hearts and minds. For some, a career provides a paycheck that supports other passions. Identifying what lights you up can help guide your decision-making by helping you identify what is important.

We asked Cristina about what is important in her life and art. She answered, "I often say, the theater, or Teatro, may not make you rich but it will give you a rich life with an abundance of profound experiences and relationships. This has been very true for me!" Knowing what is important in your life and in your art can impact your relationships, experiences, and career. What is important to you in your life and your art?

How Close Do You Need to Be to the Art to Feel Fulfilled?

In this field, we are ALL creative artists. Regardless of the specific jobs that you pursue in a creative industry, you have a relationship to the art being created. Designers, technicians, managers, production assistants: all of us are members of an artistic community. With that said, how close do you want to be to the art?

Cristina reminds us that

> Every artist has their own unique path to discover. There is no "one way" or "right way." For me, I had to experience being on the road to realize that I actually valued living in my home city, but that was after many years of travelling for work. It's so important to remember that each experience and opportunity informs the next. That is the beauty of a creative life. We have choices.

For Cristina, fulfillment in the art meant being close to the art and close to her community.

Just because others may see their art in one way, it does not mean that is how you will feel fulfilled. Find inspiration from them but resist the urge to compare yourselves to your peers, colleagues, mentors, inspirations, and creative partners. Keep it personal and really focus on what YOU need. How close do you need to be to the art to feel fulfilled?

Why Are You Drawn toward a Creative Industry, and What Do You Need from That Industry to Stay Inspired?

Of all the jobs that you could have selected, you decided to make a living based on your passions. You were drawn to the entertainment industry, and you have your own unique reasons for it. This passion can fade when it becomes our job, and keeping that passion alive is a balance between remembering what you love about the industry and staying inspired to continue working in it.

Cristina encourages that the best way to stay inspired is to establish a

> Daily Ritual. Your passion(s) in life may come and go, ebb and flow. And that's okay. Not every job or project will be of the goose bump and heart-fluttering sort, but as you travel through a creative profession, I can guarantee it will be rich and rewarding. Aim to create daily rituals for yourself that keep you connected to your

work. Draw, sketch, sing, dance, perform a monologue in your living room. Keep your creative spirit alive!

Cristina also suggests that you immerse yourself in your art, stay open, and see everything.

Staying grounded in why you chose – and continue to choose – your career path can make decision-making easier and get you through challenging moments. Creating practices for tapping into creativity and joy is an essential part of career sustainability. Why are you drawn toward a creative industry, and what do you need from that industry to stay inspired?

What Lifestyle Do You Want?

When choosing a creative occupation, think about the lifestyle associated with not only the specific job but also the greater industry. For example, if you love adventure and unpredictability, then the film industry might be for you. If you love to work with the same team but on different projects, look into a design firm. If you want to make your own schedule and be your own boss, consider becoming a freelance artist. Sometimes it is as simple as: Do you want your office to also be your car? Do you like to work at night? Do you get seasick? (If yes, you might reconsider a cruise ship career!)

Creative careers can involve long hours and often – but not always – require weekend and evening work. Your leisure activity can also be the same as your job: people in the theater are expected to see a lot of theater, and people who work in television have to keep up on current shows. Theater Technical Manager Weston Keifer sums it up best: "This career is more than a career; it's a lifestyle. There are so many paths you can go down, and it is up to you to forge your own way to success."

Like many aspects of our careers, our lifestyle goals will change over time. This is healthy and normal. It may mean that the way you engage in a creative career may shift as you move through your life. If you are an artist who needs more stability due to life circumstances, it may be time to pause your freelance employment and look for another job with benefits and a predictable schedule. If you are an artist who feels called to create meaningful work outside of your current 9-to-5 job, you may need to close that chapter in order to start a new one.

In this book, we'll talk about money. We'll talk about contracts, setting boundaries, and advocating for yourself. Thinking about your relationship to financial security, stability, and other lifestyle considerations is a healthy and necessary part of working in creative fields. A sustainable vocation is one that fits with your personal goals.

Career Entry Points

There are so many different career entry points, and all of them can lead to successful and sustainable careers. Of course, all creative professionals engage in some form of training. This is the most common entry point into our careers, when we decide we want to learn more about our passion in some sort of educational experience.

For many, this is a combination of formal education combined with hands-on work-based learning. These can happen consecutively, or simultaneously. Some people move straight from high school into training opportunities and the creative workforce, and some may come to the field later, after other jobs and vocations. We will be discussing all these pathways in this book.

Creative careers are sometimes a second career, when the passion for being an artist encourages one to shift gears and start a new path. At this point, you may choose to return to school for an additional degree or begin to work in the field doing hands-on learning. Know that entertainment utilizes so many skillsets that you will surely bring transferable skills from your previous jobs into your new line of work.

Career Guidebook Worksheets

Throughout this guidebook, you'll explore different parts of your career at the end of each chapter through interactive worksheets. By the end, you'll see your career in tangible and accountable steps. Having a plan can greatly reduce stress and fear of the unknown.

The worksheets for this chapter are titled "Artist Statement" and "My Creative Why." Laying this foundation will help you get the most out of the rest of the book, and each activity will build upon another. Sketching out your goals and dreams will help you dive into the practical information that follows in the subsequent chapters.

Creative artists are visual learners. If you can see it, then it is possible. Creative visualization is very effective for goal-setting which will highlight your personal values. Over time, these worksheets can be revisited and updated, as you enter new phases or seasons on your path. Declaring your aspirations into the universe can be the first step in making them a reality.

Introduction to Design and Technical Careers in Entertainment ◆ 13

Figure 1.1 Artist Statement.

Source: Created by Jessica Champagne Hansen using resources from Freepik.com and Macrovector.

Artist Statement

Description

There are common threads and essentials truths that make you a unique artist. Putting these truths on paper is a powerful first step toward a clearer path.

Fill in the blanks below to complete each statement.

I am a _____ artist.

My artistic style is _____

I hope that my art will change _____
_____

I am inspired by _____

My mentor(s) is/are _____

My approach to art is _____
_____

I want my art to _____
_____

My connection to my art is _____
_____

My artistic ritual is _____
_____

Follow Up

Revisit this text over your professional journey. Some statements will be constant over the length of your career, while others will shift to reflect different seasons in your life.

Figure 1.2 My Creative Why.

Source: Created by Jessica Champagne Hansen using resources from Freepik.com and Macrovector.

My Creative Why

Description

Before we investigate and analyze your career, take a moment to remember your "why." Our "why" is an anchor for our exploration and a constant reminder of where we started. Fill in the blanks below to complete each statement.

I make art because…	My heart in the art is…
I make art for myself because…	I make art for others because…

2

Creative Industry Profiles

Industry Profile Overview

This book focuses on the major employment sectors for people trained in entertainment design and technology. These sectors are theater, live entertainment, television and film, theme parks, tours, cruise ships, corporate and industrial design, and design firms.

In this chapter, we'll provide an overview of each of these fields through the eyes of working professionals, who have agreed to become de-facto "mentors" for each of you. For each sector, we provide a general overview of employment opportunities, benefits, and challenges, as well as ways you can build your skills in preparation for their line of work. We'll also explore how freelancing works and talk about allied fields.

As you read each description, consider if this is the field that not only interests you but also suits your lifestyle goals. The entertainment industry is ever-evolving and trends in employment change and can also vary in different regions of the country and internationally. View these profiles as an invitation to do further research into fields and jobs that intrigue you.

Freelance (or "Gig") Work

Let's take a moment to talk about gigs. Almost all of you will experience some form of freelance, or "gig," work during your career. There are major benefits to freelancing; who doesn't want to be their own boss? However, freelance employment has its own challenges.

Freelancers are hired on a project-by-project basis and are usually paid in lump sums without taxes withheld. This means the initial paycheck may be high, but freelancers have to be diligent about setting aside enough money to pay their taxes at the end of the year or quarterly. Gig employment also means you might not know where your next paycheck is coming from; some freelancers describe their employment as "feast or famine," with periods of high earning followed by a lull. Financial literacy and smart budgeting are key. Don't worry, we'll talk more about financial management in the next chapters.

So why do people choose freelance life? Sound Designer Corinne Corrillo shares,

> When I took the leap into freelance design, I was coming from a full-time theater design position in a regional theater. I liked that my job gave me reliable income, vacation, and medical benefits, but after a few seasons I was feeling artistically stunted. Working with the same collaborators on uninspiring productions was becoming monotonous.

As a freelancer, Corinne saw her options expand. Suddenly, she could work on live theater, film, TV, commercials, special events, new media, weddings, projects for private clients, and more! Every day and every gig can be different.

However, freelancers often have to balance the jobs that pay well with jobs that are creatively exciting. Corinne says, "I took on some audio engineer gigs to make ends meet. Then, I could take on smaller shows that fulfilled me artistically. I also taught sound design courses at universities, which led to more jobs." Even a gig that's just meant to pay the bills can lead to new creative opportunities.

The benefits of working as a freelancer include the flexibility of making your own schedule and having a high degree of independence. You can partially work from home, work on multiple projects at a time, and take on a variety of clients in a multitude of entertainment fields. But all of this requires excellent project management skills, Corinne notes: "organization is key. I cannot stress enough how important it is to keep an organized calendar, check your email and respond promptly. Paperwork will be your lifeline to juggling multiple projects at the same time."

Successful freelancers need to be entrepreneurs, skilled at authentic self-promotion and hustling for their next gig. "It is so important to nurture your contacts because you usually get jobs from people who have firsthand knowledge of your work," says Corinne. "Networking is a necessity. Go to shows, join the design team after tech, attend theater conferences and join online theater groups. You never know what new contact will get you your next big gig!" This cycle never ends, but it does get easier the longer that you have worked in your field.

There are drawbacks to freelancing. Corinne shares,

> My personal life did take a hit. Learning to juggle life along with a budding career is a challenge. It is possible to make your personal life a priority, but draw that line quickly and don't forget to make time for yourself! Running around the city or country can take a toll on you physically and mentally.

But as exhausting as this may be, Corinne says that the joy of working with other artists at a variety of jobs is artistically fulfilling. She adds, "make sure your car always has a full tank of gas, because the hustle is real!"

As we discuss the many career options within the broader entertainment field, keep in mind that the majority of jobs for designers and technicians in each of the sectors below will be in freelance employment, as opposed to salary or full-time, hourly employment. Generally, designers are more likely to be freelancers, and technicians can be either freelance or full-time/part-time regular employment. However, there are exceptions in each area. Ask your mentors, educators, and colleagues about their experiences and research job postings in your field to learn more about the different options!

Theater Careers

Live theater is the origin of almost all other forms of entertainment, and there is a special magic in it. Many of us fell in love with our art forms through the magic of theater, which unfolds live for the audience, with the designers seated beside them, the stage manager in the booth, and the technicians staged in the wings. As a Lighting Designer Ann E. McMills says, "when you are lucky enough to have a career in theater, you know you've found something special. I always come back home to theater."

Types of theaters include large regional theaters, touring houses, community theaters, small professional theaters, and summer stock. Some are for-profit, and some operate as non profit, mission-driven organizations. They have a variety of relationships with local unions, ranging from fully nonunion spaces to theaters where nearly every design and technician position requires union membership.

Get to know your area or the area where you'd like to work through online research and, most importantly, getting out and seeing shows in your community. Know the names of the theaters and the type of work that they produce. You'll often work your way from smaller to larger venues as your work experience and network develop; so don't overlook the small theaters in your community. Often, their work is innovative and allows for more risk and experimentation than the larger institutions! Remember, too, that the theater community can be a small world, which makes networking easier. Ann says, "Theater is filled with good people, meaningful work, great community, and fulfilling art."

There are many paths to a professional career in theater, with varying degrees of autonomy, stability, and creativity. For example, someone interested in lighting could pursue a career as an independent, freelance lighting designer, or could become a lighting technician at a regional theater. A lighting designer can work with many different theaters in a given year, and might not know where their next gig is coming from—but they will have a degree of creative freedom and autonomy a technician does not have. The technician may work through a union contract and will likely have a more predictable schedule, income, and benefits. Both are rewarding careers with similar skillsets, but with very different lifestyles.

Theater training is vast and varied, and the level of education required to work in theater varies by position. There is a school, program, institute, and organization for every discipline in the field. Technician positions may require specific certifications, and some (but not all) require an Associate's or Bachelor's degree. Designers often choose to pursue a Master's in their discipline, finding value in the network of collaborators you gain in a graduate school setting and the opportunities that are available for teaching at a university.

Another popular training ground and networking opportunity is summer stock, a repertory theater model where multiple productions are running at once. It is fast-paced and provides opportunities for learning and gaining skills. Ann says,

> Summer stock is the key to networking and advanced training while you are in school. Nothing changes you quite like summer stock and the people you meet will shape your career. You will walk in the door a student, and out a professional!

Note that while summer stock and other forms of theater training have often been unpaid or grossly underpaid, there is a growing call for apprentices and interns to be paid fairly for their labor. This is closely tied to equity, diversity, and inclusion in the field, as the established system of low or no wages for training opportunities is inherently inequitable. We'll explore this more in Section "Work-Based Professional Training: Internships and Apprenticeships" in Chapter 3.

The theater requires an integration of both hard and soft skills. It is a collaborative art form and requires exceptional communication, empathy, and resilience. Ann notes the importance of "staying organized, being good with people, and having a sense of humor. Don't be afraid to show a little personality!" There are also plenty of hard skills, especially in Ann's field of lighting, such as "paperwork, software, focusing, follow spots, programming." The theater is always innovating, so learning new skills will be a part of your work.

The drawbacks of working in theater as a freelancer include seasonal work, slowly working up to management or design positions, limited budgets, and long hours. Live theater also pays significantly less, in general, than the next sectors we'll discuss. However, we like Ann's take on this:

> You might have heard that you won't make a lot of money. Well, I don't believe that. Maybe you're not making Wall Street money, but I always say, "if you love what you do, the money will follow." It can sometimes take a while as a freelancer for your career to get to that place, but you can make a very comfortable living in theater. So, do what makes you happy; if you love your work, the success will follow.

Remember, too, that you can choose to work in multiple sectors, balancing your theater gigs with work in fields that generally pay more. Some people do this for their entire career, while others move solely into theater as their reputation is established and their rates start to rise.

Television and Film Careers

Many people dream of television and film careers: the glamour of a working set and your name on the credits, ... the bright lights, celebrities, and big budgets. Television and film Art Director Chris Hansen says,

> There is a brief moment of awe when you step into a world that was just lines in a script. In that moment, you feel such accomplishment knowing how many people and how much hard work went into creating something so magical.

If you're thinking of a career in this field, however, don't forget the long hours, the high stress, and the sacrifices you make in this field. That is the full package when choosing a life in film and television, one of the largest fields of entertainment.

Today, in the era of new media and streaming, content is created and shared across many platforms, leading to a wide variety of job options. Designers and technicians can work for a production studio, for a network, or with rental houses that support the industry. The field is vast, and there are many opportunities to be a part of the "movie magic."

Typically, jobs in television and film production are freelance and require union membership. If you are a union member, there are benefits like retirement and health insurance, which make independent contracting more stable. However, there are jobs available that are nonunion, including full-time employment with a studio or other company.

There are a lot of entry points into film and television, and not all of them require a college or graduate degree. Chris says,

> When I am hiring, I tend to look for those with training in theater or film. That doesn't mean that you need to have a degree. There are many different paths to success in this industry. You need to have a solid creative foundation.

Creativity is key, and Chris, like many in the field, looks for people who can:

> Dream and create a world that inspires an emotion, first, and then worry about how to build it. You can't be bogged down by the

reality of creating something before first exploring the unknown and testing the limits of your creativity.

Think about your approach to pushing boundaries, and seek opportunities to explore your creativity and develop your craft.

As creative as film and television occupations are, Chris explains that the industry requires just as many "left-brain" skills as "right-brain." He says, "You need to know a little bit about everything from art history to construction; from management to budgeting." He adds that in his position, he oversees many departments and aspects of the production and often needs to be everywhere at once, requiring organization and prioritization:

> At the end of the day, you need to work within a budget and schedule to make sure that everyone has the time and information that they need. In TV, a full shoot can happen in less than seven days.

This is, after all, why they call it show business: it's a combination of creativity and the skills to realize the vision on time, and within budget.

Making films and television shows is a dream career for many, and there are a lot of benefits. You can work with comparatively large budgets, tap into exciting projects, and may feel like every day is a new adventure. The fields are always at the forefront of new technologies, so you will be a part of the future of entertainment – and need to constantly learn new skills to keep up!

Film work can take you all over the world or keep you close to home if you happen to live in a market with a lot of production. A film project can be anywhere from a single day of work in your home city to several months away from home working on-site. If you enjoy traveling, film can give you a great opportunity to see the world.

Working in television has a more predictable schedule than film, and a seasonal flow. You are likely to have a few months of intense work, followed by a hiatus (or unemployment, if the show is ending). If you are lucky to be on a popular show, you may be able to work for multiple years on the same project, with a consistent team. However, while television used to have a standard number of episodes which would guarantee a longer employment period, in today's new media world a television show may only film eight episodes, or fewer.

Behind the magic of the lights and the cameras, there are disadvantages to a career among the stars. Chris admits,

> This is a hard industry and I would be lying if I told you that this job was for everyone or that I love my job every second of the day. The pay can be good, but it is not uncommon to work 12 hours a day every day. TV shows are becoming more like feature films so now you'll find yourself also working weekends, which rarely happened just a few years ago.

After that intensity, too, comes long breaks where you'll need to tap into your network to find your next gig. Chris says,

> There is a chance that you might go for months without work and this is when "who you know" comes into play, since most of the time you get your next job based on word of mouth. It is nerve-wracking to not know when or where your next job will be.

And finally, Chris shares that every project that you work on will likely have a whole different crew. He says that this is like being a "chameleon, where you adapt to each new working group and find ways to mesh together."

With all these drawbacks in the field, Chris jokes,

> Why would anyone choose this path?! Given all the stress, work and instability of the job, the moment you walk onto a set that came together in a week, that transports you to a new world, that makes it worth it. You created the impossible and brought a vision to life.

Film and television capture the imagination of millions of viewers and provide a rewarding career for many creative professionals.

Theme Park Careers

How amazing is it to create an interactive world where guests become a character in the story? Theme Parks are rich with exciting forms of entertainment, from themed lands to immersive rides, large-scale theatrical productions, and engaging parades. The theme park field also includes zoos, water parks, and aquariums, all of which often utilize creative professionals to design immersive environments. If you love theme parks, you might consider one of the many careers available in this industry for technician and design professionals.

Theme park jobs are often stable, steady, and salaried, with health insurance, retirement, and benefits. You could have a consistent work location or be relocated for a period of time to work at specific parks, with exciting opportunities abroad. Theme park projects have larger budgets than most theater productions and come with interesting design challenges. For example, unlike theater, theme parks are built to last for years, and the guests are able to get up close to see every detail of your work.

Josh Steadman, Theme Park Art Director and Designer, says,

> my advice to anyone looking to work in the theme park design industry is to start by working in an actual theme park. I spent my summers working as an attractions host and selling park tickets. I learned theme park operations, guest flow and basic park operations so I could be a great theme park designer.

Hands-on training at a theme park will help prepare you for the unique design and technical opportunities of the field.

Theme park professionals come from a variety of educational backgrounds. Many studied theater and often move to themed entertainment from an initial theater career. Others, like Josh, have a visual arts background: "The years practicing drawing and attending critiques [in art school] provided me with a foundation of design and illustration that was essential to my knowledge of art direction in theme parks." Regardless of your pathway in any entertainment field, having a working understanding of art and design is crucial.

Collaboration and working with a team are other important skills for this line of work. Josh says that this can be a challenge, as many visual artists are used to working alone or in a private studio. Theme park jobs also require "hard work and discipline," says Josh. "Experience is a great teacher, which takes time and failure. Always be teachable and willing to learn no matter what stage you are in your career. It is a lifelong pursuit."

Working in themed entertainment can have drawbacks, but it all depends on your perspective. As an artist, you will follow the aesthetic defined by the park and corporation. Design is often "by committee," which can be limiting for certain artistic styles. Many theme parks are corporate settings, with dress codes and business guidelines. The work often requires non-disclosure agreements and the environment can be stressful with big budgets, limited time, and high stakes. However, if you love the magic of these environments, these can be tremendously rewarding careers.

Touring Careers

Touring Audio Engineer Ashley Diaz sets the scene:

> "Go on tour, they said; it would be fun, they said." This is your 3am mantra as you coil 150 feet of cable as fast as you can. You pack the trucks, run to the bus, grab some clean clothes, speed-shower in the venue (if the venue has showers), run back to the bus, hop in a bunk, and get three hours of sleep only to repeat it again. Sound fun?

To Ashley, yes, it does! She says,

> Touring is a beast and you learn rather quickly if it is right for you. You must love what you do because after a week of getting two to three hours a night of sleep you are running on passion and coffee. That being said, I love what I do.

Tours can be for live theater, industrial tradeshows, concerts, other live entertainment, or events. If you love traveling, this is an excellent career option – and your professional network grows at every tour stop. Says Ashley,

> For some tours you live on a bus and are in a city one or two days before you move to the next location; these are known as one-nighter tours. Another type of tour involves living in a hotel, or even being able to rent an apartment, for longer periods, typically a month or two.

Living and working on the road is an exciting experience.

The best training ground for a profession in touring is the theater, where you will develop technical skills, communication strategies, and problem-solving. There are fewer educational requirements than in other fields, except in some specialist positions. Ashley states,

> If you are interested in pursuing a career in touring, you must have a basic knowledge of your craft and be comfortable with your skills. Having knowledge of other departments is crucial, and being able to communicate clearly will make your experience much smoother. Also, you must be able to keep your cool in high-stress situations.

If you are thinking of going on tour, you might try summer stock theater or other repertory theater models to prepare for touring jobs, which employ similar skills.

There is a lot of variety in touring, for instance, sometimes the tour comes to your main location, and you join the team as a local technician. In general, touring is a life that involves living out of suitcases and being away from home for long periods. Ashley says,

> You will find yourself writing reminders to call your loved ones. Being away from home isn't always easy and it can take a toll. Whatever fatigue you are fighting doesn't matter: curtain is at 8pm and you better be on your game. Things malfunction and you have to be able to think fast and fix the problem on the spot.

If you have an adventurous spirit and love the adrenaline rush of problem-solving, it may be time to pack your suitcase and hit the road!

Cruise Ship Careers

If you love to travel and work within unique parameters, designing and being a technician on the open seas could be for you. Aaron Jackson, Scenic and Entertainment Designer, describes the field of cruise ship entertainment as "Exotic destinations, amazing cuisine and adventure on the high seas!" It will not be a permanent vacation, though, as you are there to work. However, as Aaron says, "when you are having your morning coffee overlooking the ancient city walls of Valetta, Malta, working seems like a small price to pay."

Cruise ships have endless types of entertainment, all of which require teams of professionals. There are full-scale live theater productions, comedy shows, ice skating performances, acrobats, dance shows, and more. Aaron says, "Cruise ships are very competitive with their entertainment, constantly looking for the 'next big thing' and idea. They are at the forefront of new technologies and creative innovation, and more importantly, generally have the budget to back them up." There are so many opportunities to try something new, travel somewhere new, and practice new skills.

If you are hired as a designer, you will only be on the ship for a cruise or two for installation and tech. You will be able to experience the ship as a passenger. Technicians, however, have a different experience, as Aaron explains: "if you join the ship as an onboard technician, you are considered crew members, and will usually have additional duties outside the theater. Typically, contracts are six to eight months." Each cruise ship and job position is different, though, so be sure to do research before you start updating your passport.

Many people move into cruise ship careers after studying and/or working in live theater, as the skills are highly transferrable. Aaron says,

> Most ships have multiple shows that are set up and taken down every night, so you are always designing with that in mind. It can really challenge you creatively. You have to create pieces that fit into small storage and keep hanging scenery from swaying with the ship during a show.

These parameters can make for exciting and creative opportunities.

Just like touring, cruise ship careers require you to be comfortable being away from home for days or months at a time. Since you are staying on the ship, Aaron shares that cruise ship jobs are "a great way to bank away some extra savings while you travel the world."

However, there are some drawbacks to a career in cruise ship entertainment. There will be times when the excitement of travel wears off, the working hours are long, your small room feels like it is getting smaller, and you just want to stop swaying back and forth. There will be times when you do not have all the tools that you'd have on land, and, as Aaron says, "You can't always run to the hardware store when something doesn't work." He adds, "It is a fairly small, niche industry so it can be hard to break into from a design standpoint, but if you are able to get in, it will be worth the effort."

Design Firms and Corporate Design

Employment with a design firm and with corporate clients opens doors to work for retail stores, cruise ships, trade shows, concerts, museums, exhibits, theme parks, special events, and more. Design firms serve many industries but have two primary types of projects: permanent projects and temporary projects. Permanent projects include retail stores, restaurants, theme park rides, museum exhibits, and performance venues. Temporary projects include trade shows, private events like film premieres, live shows for theme parks, and seasonal events.

Working with a firm provides a consistent paycheck and more standard hours, vacation time, and benefits. Jennifer Goldstein, Lighting Designer and President of Radiance Lightworks, Inc., explains, "as a freelancer, or independent designer, your bandwidth may be limited by your ability to be in one place at a time. At a firm, many designers work on each project, allowing everyone to work on many projects simultaneously." Your training will be an asset to your colleagues, and you will also receive on-the-job cross-training from colleagues with different specializations. This is a great way to stay flexible and work in numerous fields, all while maintaining some balance and consistency. As Jennifer says, "the benefit of working for a design firm is variety."

Many firms, especially those working in themed entertainment, tend to hire designers trained in theater; however, designers do come from a variety of backgrounds. To be a competitive applicant to a design firm, Jennifer shares, "you should be able to use drafting software and have a portfolio with select projects showing your skills. Most firms emphasize and lean heavily on production paperwork to support the design."

Jennifer notes that soft skills like communication and professionalism are critical in these career fields: "Those are 'make it or break it' skills required to work at a design firm. Clients expect to see clearly written emails, designers with level heads, and professional use of language." Hands-on, work-based learning such as internships and apprenticeships are great opportunities to build your knowledge of professionalism and collaboration. If you are in a formal training program such as a college or university, consider taking courses in language and communication to build your written and verbal skills.

There are many benefits to working in a design firm and with corporate clients. Jennifer breaks it down into three main points:

> First, everyone can contribute their unique skills to a project. Second, there is a lot of opportunity for growth and discovery. Often, designers will come into the firm with an interest in a particular area, such as concerts, but over time, their interests may shift to museum exhibits or trade shows. Third, you always have backup. This means you can make time for your personal life. Responsibility for projects may be handed off between team members, allowing you to take vacation or deal with emergencies that inevitably come up.

Other than these personal benefits, depending on the project, there are usually large budgets and fun tech toys in this line of work. The projects are exciting, and you will get to practice your skills working within a brand.

The corporate environment is not for everyone. Think about your comfort level with a set dress code and the requirement to sign a nondisclosure agreement. There are long hours and potential required travel for certain projects. Each firm is different, and you may be brought onto the team on an individual project basis, so you will not receive all the benefits of being a full-time employee. Design firms focus on teamwork and collaboration, which may not be a good match if you prefer working independently.

Education Careers

Careers in entertainment are exciting because they lead us down pathways that we never knew existed, and we suddenly find ourselves far from our starting place in new roles and fields. Our positions can also become hybrid, where you are working at the intersection of your unique skills and experiences. If you enjoy teaching and mentorship, you may consider one of the many careers that combine education and creative disciplines.

Ashleigh Akilah Rucker is a Program Supervisor for a touring educational theater program, which means that she provides everything from artistic oversight to project management support. She says, "I am described as a Program Supervisor, but beneath the surface you will find an artistic director, a manager for artists, an educator and a community advocate." She notes that everything she brings to her hybrid career are skills she learned in her theater training: "This work requires creative problem-solving, critical thinking and working as a collaborative team member. You need strong communication skills and training in equity, diversity and inclusion."

Many arts educators find themselves pulled to teaching because of a desire to make a bigger and more lasting impact. Technical Manager and educator Weston Keifer says, "In my journey, I discovered that I wanted to give back. I had amazing teachers and mentors and wanted to be sure the next generation of stagehands had those same benefits." Similarly, Ashleigh shares that the biggest draw for her in this work is

> Knowing that I'm making a difference in a young person's life. Not only are we using the arts to educate, we're introducing the art form of theater to new audiences, most of which are communities of color. So as a Black woman, I get to literally set the stage to authentically represent the audiences we serve.

She encourages you to "be intentional about your work and the community that you build. Surround yourself with people who make you better."

A career in arts education or teaching may not come with the name recognition of a successful design career; as Ashley says, "This is not always flashy or fiscally lucrative work." Weston agrees that this path can be tough. However, as he puts it, "a life in theater [education] is one of the most rewarding and the most challenging you can choose." Ashleigh adds, "It's a wonderfully rewarding world of hardworking creatives who use the arts to educate, challenge, and entertain."

Time to Reflect

You've heard from many people across a variety of careers in entertainment. Take a second to pause and think about which of their stories seemed most exciting and inspiring. Are you drawn toward careers that involve travel? How much does money and financial stability influence your decision-making? Do you want to be a part of a team, or work independently?

Imagine your skillsets and passions and perhaps your pathway will be at the intersection. One of the most powerful tools for career development is letting your curiosity guide you. Don't be afraid to pursue multiple interests and develop *all* of your talents and look for a job that speaks to all of them!

Creative Industry Profiles ◆ 31

Figure 2.1 Career Vision Board.

Source: Created by Jessica Champagne Hansen using resources from Freepik.com and Macrovector.

Career Vision Board

Description

As creative artists, we use words, images, and themes in our work. Now, use them to design your future on top of this template. Draw, doodle, cut, paste, color, and get crafty!

- My goals
- What I am grateful for
- My dreams
- My motivation
- My creativity
- My Career Vision
- My skills
- My inspiration
- What I love to do
- Where I want to go
- What I want

Follow Up

Keep this vision board in your workspace, as a constant reminder of the big picture. Each day, you will manifest these goals into your work.

3

Education, Degrees, and Training

Educational Pathways

Choosing your educational pathway is one of the first major career decisions you'll make. There are many degrees and certificate options for creative professionals, as well as hands-on training opportunities like internships and apprenticeships. There is no "one size fits all" solution to education and training; it's a personal decision that should serve your professional and lifestyle goals.

If you're still debating whether to pursue your master's or enter the workforce after your current training is complete, then read on. This chapter will outline a variety of training options, along with the pros and cons of each.

First, we'll explore degree and certification options in formal higher education programs. Many professionals start their post-high-school education in a college, university, or technical training institute setting. We'll discuss the differences among Associate of Arts (AA), Bachelor of Arts (BA), Bachelor of Fine Arts (BFA), Master of Arts (MA), and Master of Fine Arts (MFA) degrees, and alternative higher education opportunities.

DOI: 10.4324/9781003052227-5

> **A note on Conservatories:** Another option – conservatory programs – allow students to focus their studies almost entirely on their major. They are designed to be one to three years in duration and can be either independent institutions or located on the campus of a community college, college, or university. Conservatory programs are primarily focused on performance training, so we won't be exploring them in depth in this book.

Next, we'll talk about work-based training options. These are hands-on educational opportunities that take place in professional settings. The most common work-based programs are internships and apprenticeships. Some are paid, some are not, and some make you pay to participate (more on that later!).

Remember that your educational journey will continue throughout your life, even after you've received your degree or completed an official training program. New technologies and changing trends mean that creative professionals have to continue learning throughout their career to keep up with the industry. Staying competitive means committing to lifelong learning!

Making Choices and the Value of Creative Education

What do you do with a BA in Theater? SO MANY THINGS. Regardless of what you might hear from family members or guidance counselors, there are many, many rewarding and sustainable careers – both within the creative industries and outside of them – that you can pursue after you complete your education in a creative field. (Flip to Chapter 9 if you want to learn about transferrable skills!) While it's normal, and healthy, to think critically about how you may utilize a degree or certificate, don't let uninformed outside opinions discourage you from pursuing creative education.

We asked Dr. Sergio Ramirez, Associate Dean of Admissions and Student Services in the Theater department at a private four-year university, about the value of creative education and what advice he gives to prospective students. "Pursuing education in the arts is not always easy and requires persistence," he says.

> The amount of personal struggle and sacrifice many artists share should not go unnoticed. This career path is not for the faint

of heart. Yet, the love and personal fulfillment one gains from engaging in such art supersedes any amount of sacrifice.

For those who feel called to creative careers, the joy and satisfaction you find in your work can be your strongest motivator.

However, that doesn't mean you don't need to think deeply about your educational choices and consider whether an opportunity will support your financial, artistic, and lifestyle goals. Remember: there's no "right answer" here that will guarantee success. Sergio explains,

> An abundance of resources does not guarantee success. While resources and opportunities are key towards supporting a student's professional ambition, no amount of these will do any good if one does not actively pursue and engage in the process of risk, curiosity, and experimentation by doing the work.

This is liberating, because it means that you hold the key to making the best of your training with your own ambition and drive. Sergio encourages, "If the fire and determination to share your story and your craft is strong – you can always find a space to do so."

Sergio notes that students of color and those from marginalized backgrounds have additional considerations. He says,

> Through my own experience as a minority whose parents never had this opportunity, I know firsthand the immeasurable benefits one gains from a post-secondary education. There are a number of struggles or barriers, especially for students of color. The best advice I can offer is to seek out people who do what you want to do and research how people got to where they are.

Look at the faculty, guest artists, and alumni of colleges and universities you are considering. Do they reflect you, and your life experiences?

Regarding the difference between a two-year and a four-year degree, Sergio advises,

> In all honesty, the years of the degree do not matter. What matters most are the environments that students are exposed to. In a traditional four-year college setting, there are certain experiences that help shape a student's identity that cannot be replicated in other

ways. The additional benefit is the level of exposure and cultivation that takes place within that amount of time. The same can be said for a 2-year program or conservatory experience. In the end, it all comes down to what the student takes advantage of in any one experience.

Diving into campus culture and opportunities may be easier at a four-year college but is certainly possible in other environments as well!

Education is an investment in yourself. Try to quiet the voices of others – particularly those who doubt you – and find the educational options that best support you as an artist and individual.

Higher Education

Higher education refers to formal, accredited programs you enter after receiving your high school diploma or GED (General Education Development) degree. Enrolling in a higher education institution provides opportunities beyond just taking classes. It brings you into a community of peers, mentors, and professionals, setting you up for success in your profession.

A major benefit of education, no matter the type or level, is the networking potential it can provide. Stage manager, production manager, producer, and educator Joel Veenstra credits his experiences in higher education with his wide range of professional opportunities. He says,

> In college, a guest speaker shared, "The entertainment industry is hard to get into, but it is not impossible. I got into it, so you can too, if you want to and you work hard toward that goal." That was just mind boggling to me, transformative even: it not only was a potential career, but it was specifically an option *for me*. Someone I was now in direct contact with had already walked that road and was sharing insights on how to follow in their path.

That small moment changed his whole calling.

Higher education is a time to both experiment and find your focus areas. Joel shares,

> In undergrad, I was able to get a sampling, or smorgasbord, of all of the different options that were available. Then, grad school

helped me refine and focus my skillset, specifically for stage management, which best aligned with my abilities and goals.

College has more to offer than a "piece of paper." Pursuing degrees and/or certificates helps you to develop soft and hard skills, allows you to explore career options, and introduces you to working professionals. For many, the relationships formed with peers and instructors during their education continue throughout their professional lives.

Community Colleges

Community colleges are affordable higher education institutions, focused on preparing students for the workforce and/or for transfer to four-year colleges and universities. They offer flexible learning opportunities that can lead to both degrees and the receipt of certificates. Community colleges have different degree types, but the most common for the entertainment field is an AA degree. If you are able to attend full-time, AA degrees take about two years to complete.

The programs of study at a community college are created with job opportunities in mind, especially if they focus on Career Technical Education (CTE). CTE certificate and degree programs respond to industry trends and demands and often engage industry professionals as instructors or on advisory committees.

Flexibility and cost are two of the main benefits of pursuing a degree and/or certificate at a community college. Classes are offered online, at night, and on weekends, which can make it easier to work part-time while you are pursuing your goals. Classes are often smaller at a community college than at a large four-year institution, and there is rolling admission so you can begin in spring semester, or even take one short-term course if desired. If you are still figuring out what you'd like to focus on, community college is a great time to explore, and many students find it an easier transition from high school or returning to college after a break. Students can also begin taking courses at community colleges while they are under 18, and even when they are still enrolled in high school. Many students attend a community college in preparation for transfer to a four-year college or university.

They are also an economical option, as community college tuition is far lower than four-year programs. Film and television costumer Victoria

Inez Rivera started her educational journey in fashion at a community college for financial reasons, but she quickly realized the true value of the education she was receiving:

> I couldn't afford to attend a private well-known fashion institute, so I attended one of my city's community colleges. I was not only saving a tremendous amount of money, but I looked up to the instructors and professors teaching and work experience.

She also took advance of the flexibility of the community college system to discover a new passion. She remembers,

> In just days of starting classes, I got sucked into the Theater Arts department's costume program. I took every costume course, participated in everything and found myself at a crossroads. Do I stay in fashion or pursue my new love of costuming?

Victoria realized she could apply many of the skills and creative elements of her fashion education to costuming and ended up graduating with multiple degrees, as well as several certificates.

Certificates in the community college system are focused on achievement in specific skills, such as Tailoring or Scenic Painting. They can be pursued either instead of or in addition to a degree. These certificates vary in the number of classes required and by topic but typically take less time to complete than a degree. Students can "stack" numerous certificates to customize their education based on their job goals.

There are some drawbacks for community college training. There are more lower-division courses than upper-division courses, meaning courses tend to be more general than specialized. For students who do plan to transfer to a four-year school, sometimes not all of the college credits earned at a community college will count toward your Bachelor's degree. The campus experience at a community college can be different, as there is rarely on-campus housing and fewer social opportunities. Another drawback is that the flexibility of a community college can actually backfire and lead students to take more classes than they need, as they become more involved in department productions and exploring classes.

However, sometimes that flexibility is exactly what students need to achieve their goals on their ideal timeline. While still pursuing her AA degree, Victoria worked her way from a production assistant on big-budget TV shows and films to a position at a union costume house as a stock costumer – all while taking one or two courses each semester. Victoria shares,

> The two biggest milestones on my journey came within the same year! I was inducted as a union member in the industry with my job title as a Costumer and I finally graduated with my AA degree in Theater Arts with an emphasis in Costumes! This pathway I took to achieve these goals wasn't the norm, easy or fast. My achievements came at a later age than most. I was working in my preferred industry, sworn into the union and obtained my degree all on top of turning thirty that year!

Note from Jess, a Community College Professor: If a community college sounds like the right choice for you, here is some advice. Some people believe that a lower tuition price means a lower-quality education. That's false. I work with incredibly talented and dedicated faculty, staff, and students at my institution. I also highly recommend the incredible student services available at a community college, especially Academic Counseling. Meeting with them every semester will help you stay on track toward graduation. A little planning and support will get you to your goal, just like Victoria did!

Undergraduate Programs: Colleges and Universities

Undergraduate degrees are typically designed around a four-year timeline and are offered through colleges and universities. A liberal arts college is typically smaller than a university, with fewer courses and a focus on a well-rounded education for all students, regardless of their major. Universities can be public (run by the state or local government) or private (independent for-profit or nonprofit institutions). A university is generally larger, with more options for specialization; many actually have separate "schools" with different admission processes for each. Class sizes at a university can be quite large and may be taught by research assistants or graduate students instead of professors. Universities may have more resources and larger programs, but colleges may provide more access to professors; every program is different.

There are many benefits to pursuing undergraduate education. It's a valuable time to develop relationships with fellow students and faculty. After graduation, you will also be a part of the alumni network, with connections to colleagues from different graduating years. And some, but not all, jobs in entertainment require the completion of an undergraduate degree.

Both colleges and universities offer degrees in various areas such as theater, film, television, and more. BA and BFA are the most commonly awarded degrees for undergraduates planning to pursue careers in technical entertainment. They are typically designed for full-time study, with some room for part-time jobs or internships. Both degrees will combine arts courses with general education courses for a well-rounded higher education experience, but in a BA program, you will spend about 50–60% of your time taking classes specific to your artistic discipline, compared to roughly 70% of your courses in a BFA program. BFA programs are often viewed as more competitive and can require an additional portfolio review, audition, or interview process for admission. Some schools offer both a BA and BFA track, where students in each program may take the same courses but have different requirements and, often, levels of access to opportunities like designing for a mainstage program or working with a visiting designer.

Costs vary greatly and can be offset by scholarship options, work study, and other financial aid options. Many creative individuals dislike thinking about money, but money needs to be a factor in your educational decisions. Remember that while some creative industry jobs come with high six-figure incomes, the vast majority do not. Taking on student loan debt is a viable option for affording college, but you should tread carefully and be aware of how long repayment would take based on what you are likely to make post-college.

Each college program is unique, and selecting the right one for you is a big decision. If possible, visit the campus, take a tour, and speak directly with faculty and students. You can also dive into research: look up their course offerings, their alumni and what type of work they are doing, their faculty, and the professional work they participate in off-campus. Other factors to consider are opportunities to study abroad, campus diversity, and demonstrated commitment to anti-racist practice, religious and spiritual communities, extracurricular activities and student clubs, and whether you prefer a campus with an active Greek life (fraternity and sorority). You may also decide to attend a school in the city or area where you'd like to work post-graduation, to help make your transition from school to work more seamless. Each institution has different admissions and application process; if you're thinking of applying, create a spreadsheet to remember all the details, due dates, and requirements for the schools you are interested in.

Undergraduate program options can seem limitless. How do you choose which one is right for you? We asked Costume Specialist and Project Manager Meghan Ims for her advice. Meghan's career journey started as a biology major and Veterinary Assistant, but two costume courses in the Theater department of her community college made her realize that costuming was a viable career option. After she completed her AA in Theater with a Costume Emphasis, she asked herself a series of questions to help her choose a BFA program that was right for her:

- ◆ What kinds of experiences do I want to have in my education?
- ◆ What do I want to learn that I don't know yet?
- ◆ What is going to help me get ahead in my chosen career?

Meghan submitted six applications to the programs she felt most excited about and received two acceptance letters. She says she chose the program that "pushed my creativity and artistic voice, and where I learned the language of expression and how to communicate through different mediums." This experience was different from her two-year program, which "focused on practical foundational skills and all the necessary processes to bring a production to life." Meghan recognized where she needed to grow and chose a program that supported that:

> As contrasting as the two schools are they both gave me a balanced perspective as a theater artist. This allows me to understand the concepts being communicated through designs, while breaking down how to realistically achieve that design within the constraints of budget and construction.

Think about developing yourself as a well-rounded creative individual, with a combination of artistic skill, knowledge of our industry, and practical skills like budgeting and project management.

Undergraduate programs can be an excellent place to try new ideas, grow as an artist, and learn fundamental skills. Some people feel ready to step into the workforce post-graduation; others choose to go on to a graduate program.

Graduate School

Graduate school provides an opportunity for focused study in a specific area, after completion of an undergraduate program. Programs are roughly two to three years, but the duration can be shorter if they are pursued in tandem with an undergraduate degree (research "accelerated 4+1 degree") or longer if the student is working full-time or pursuing a more in-depth degree, such as a doctoral degree.

While graduate school has a reputation for being expensive, some programs are fully funded and free to attend, while others offer financial assistance or teaching assistantships to help offset the expense. Being a teaching assistant or instructor can be invaluable in developing both teaching and leadership skills. A graduate degree also opens doors to teach at the university level, as the majority of teaching positions in higher education require a postgraduate or terminal degree.

The most common graduate degrees related to the entertainment industry are MA and MFA. Generally, an MA in a creative discipline is focused on a more scholarly or research-based approach, and an MFA is designed to launch students into professional practice. For example, an MA in Arts Management may include the study of arts policy, leadership ethics, and organizational finance, while an MFA in Theater Management may focus more on production budgets, union negotiation, and contracts. Some graduate programs are connected to a repertory theater, production studio, or radio station, providing hands-on opportunities in a professional setting.

> **A note from Camille: I had a three-month career as an actor, immediately after I graduated with a BA in Theater. That's how long it took me to realize that while I loved acting, I actually hated *being***

> ***an actor*, from constant driving to auditions to online submissions to hours spent waiting on sets. If I had gone straight from an undergraduate study into graduate school, I would have pursued an MFA in Acting, which would have made my realization that I hated being an actor a lot more expensive. Taking time to work in the field helped me discover my passion for theater leadership and management, and my graduate degree in Arts Management helps me every day!**

Graduate school provides an opportunity to explore your creativity, hone your craft, and develop your artistic viewpoint. Holly Poe Durbin, Costume Professor and Head of Design in the Theater department of a large public university, told us,

> Earning an MFA deepened my ability and created a framework for my creativity. It helped me create a personal working system to successfully deliver large, complex projects. It also allowed my career path to be much more flexible and gave me opportunities to embrace serendipity.

A graduate degree can deepen and refine your professional practice, setting you up for career growth.

You do not need to enter a graduate program immediately after completion of your undergraduate degree. In fact, many people find value in working in their intended field before investing in graduate school, in order to get a better sense of what they still need to learn and where they might want to specialize. Holly shares,

> I was already a member of United Scenic Artists and had assisted on a Broadway show when I decided to attend graduate school. I wanted to invest in the broad and deep skills that would make me a more thoughtful, confident, and skilled designer . . . Of course, I was terrified to give up working but graduate school turned out to be the best investment I ever made in myself.

Remember that studying something and actually working in that field are very different; make sure you understand your commitment to a career path before making the investment in graduate school.

How do you decide which graduate program is right for you? Holly shared the questions she asked herself when making her graduate school decision:

- **Are the faculty people you want to study with?** Can you go through the process of personal and professional growth with them? Are you excited about their professional work, and do you believe they will be able to connect you to potential job opportunities?
- **Does the program ask you to study more than one area** (for instance scenic design and lighting design) **or does this program specialize in a single area only?** This is all about your preference and speaks to whether you are interested in being a specialist or generalist.
- **Does the curriculum focus on exactly what you want to learn?** Are you an early-career designer looking to learn new technology or a beginner who needs to develop professional methodology and expertise? Are you drawn toward a specific creative style, method of working, or type of art? The specificity of graduate programs means it's essential for you to not only understand their focus area but also your own needs as an artist and professional.

> **The URTAs: The University Resident Theatre Association has a recruiting audition and interview program for MFA candidates across more than 40 college and university theater programs, with events held in multiple locations in the United States. Holly, who serves as the president of URTA, shares, "One of the advantages of attending the URTAs is the opportunity to compare dozens of schools side-by-side. I sometimes think of the URTAs as a match-making service." If you're hoping to find an MFA program, look into attending at URTA.com.**

Training and Certificates

Professional training and certificate programs that take place outside of colleges and universities can be practical opportunities for learning new skills, either as your primary form of post-high-school education or as "upskilling" opportunities. Specialized training can help you make a career jump or qualify for new positions in management or leadership.

Specialty trainings are offered through private institutions, unions, and independent organizations. They vary greatly in cost to participate and in duration, ranging from a single day to a few months. Many provide intensive training on hard skills, such as new technology, software, and machinery. Programs can also focus on building soft skills, including management training, conflict resolution, and diversity and inclusion best practices.

What's it like to participate in an intensive, short-term training program? We asked Jane Childs, Director and Head of Faculty for the Stagecraft Institute of Las Vegas (SILV), to tell us about the participant experience at this eight-week training institute focused on entertainment technology. Jane talked about SILV's "intensive eight-to-ten-hour training days, plus evening lab sessions and attending live performances . . . Each week focuses on a different topic: digital drafting, rigging, automation, audio, lighting technology, electrics, media, consoles, and busking." Each section is taught by working professionals familiar with cutting-edge technology and who can also connect participants to networking opportunities and prospective employers.

This kind of short-term training program provides a lot of benefits in a short amount of time. The dynamic learning environment also attracts an extremely diverse group of individuals. Jane explains,

> Over the years, our students have ranged in age from teens to seniors across all experience levels, including those who are brand-new to the industry, high school graduates who want to go to work instead of college, college students of all levels, and working professionals and teachers seeking professional development. We train all of these students in the same room at the same time.

Look for programs that fill in gaps in your skillset and provide opportunities for networking. In a field where technology is constantly evolving, these programs can bring major benefits to professionals of all ages and experience levels.

Work-Based Professional Training: Internships and Apprenticeships

Work-based learning opportunities provide hands-on training in a professional setting. The most common types of work-based professional training are internships and apprenticeships. There are many benefits to these experiences, including networking, working with a mentor, diversifying the experiences on your resume, and learning through practice in the industry.

What's the difference between an internship and an apprenticeship? Unfortunately, there is little consistency in how these terms are used and what the differences are between them. Traditionally, the word "apprenticeship" implied that the apprentice would move directly into professional practice after completion of the training program, and some apprenticeships still culminate in union membership or hiring opportunities. Internships are more likely to be semester-based and can sometimes focus more on management or administration than apprenticeships. However, the names are often used interchangeably.

Internships and apprenticeships are sometimes a part of college or university studies and are taken for college credit. These opportunities tend to be designed around a school schedule, but some internships can actually be full-time and make it difficult to continue attending school while participating.

Many apprenticeships and internship opportunities involve compensation for participants, either instead of school credit or in addition to it; compensation may include regular wages, benefits such as medical insurance, housing and food, transportation, and/or other perks such as theater tickets.

However, some work-based learning opportunities either pay very little, don't pay at all, or require YOU to pay to participate! There is a major call in our industry to move away from these models, which can take advantage of early-career individuals and do lasting damage to access and diversity in our industry. If you do choose to participate in an unpaid or very low-paying internship or apprenticeship, you should be confident in its educational aspects and be aware that these opportunities perpetuate cycles of privilege. And if you feel like an "internship" is just using you for free labor, get out!

We asked Internship Program Manager and Education Director Angela Scott about the Latino Theater Company's Play at Work program, to weigh in on the benefits of workforce training for aspiring designers and technicians. She says,

> Internships and apprenticeships can be an invaluable avenue to transitioning from the academic world to a professional career. Along with gaining professional experience and building one's resume, those emerging into the field of technical arts can solidify their network and take advantage of opportunities that come their way.

It is a great way to begin the shift from education to career.

Just like finding the right school, it is important to find the right internship or apprenticeship. Angela recommends:

> researching companies, especially their mission and production history, to try to find a place that reflects your own artistic values. It's important to remember that a career in tech or design will probably entail working at multiple venues over time, and your reputation will eventually become as important as your resume. You will need that network you built through your internship or apprenticeship advocating for you.

That network can sometimes lead directly to a job: after they complete Play at Work, many of the interns and apprentices Angela works with are hired by the theater. This is very common, as former interns and apprentices have already built relationships and demonstrated their skills and work ethic over the course of their programs.

Applying for internships and apprenticeships can be nearly as stressful as applying for college and can sometimes have equally long timelines. They can also be competitive, and some early-career theater artists may start to get discouraged after applying to multiple positions. Angela encourages, "If you don't break into your dream company for your internship or apprenticeship, continue to pursue one with other companies. Eventually you will find yourself working at the place you ideally want to be."

And above all: Keep applying. Don't let your fear of the unknown hold you back. We know the stakes can feel high. Then the fear, self-doubt, and imposter syndrome set in. We see so many incredible artists actually talk themselves out of even applying! The most important thing to remember is that you are not alone. We all feel self-doubt at some point in our journey. Rely on your mentors and your colleagues for support and be brave. **Keep Applying.**

> **Note from Jess on self-doubt and vulnerability: About a year ago I confessed to my mentor that I had failed. Not just a simple mistake, like an epic fail. It was hard to share that news with them. I have looked up to them for career advice since the first day I walked into their office. After all that fear and self-doubt, they told me that this failure meant that another door would open that was MY door and that opportunities arise when the timing is right. And they were right: Here I am writing the book that was once my epic fail! I printed my mentor's email to me and it is on my office door as a daily reminder!**

If you're ready to apply but want to stand out from other applicants, get ready for a resume makeover. In Chapter 5, we will look at strategies and best practices for your career marketing materials, including your resume, cover letter, portfolio, website, and more!

The Cost of Education and Training

Education and training all come at a cost. Higher education tuition fees can add up to over $100,000 for four years of training, or more. The classes themselves are not the only cost. Training also involves materials, textbooks, resources, housing, transportation, and living expenses. There are many options for making education more affordable. Let's break them down.

Financial aid helps to pay for your higher education costs. Aid comes in the form of scholarships, student loans, fee waivers, and grants. Many financial aid opportunities are based on your field of study and location, so it is best to explore financial aid while you are also looking for the best school or training programs for you. Review the financial aid information on the institution's websites. This takes time, but it is well worth it! Sometimes a student can receive a full financial aid package to cover all their costs, but more commonly students use multiple forms of financial aid to create a package that pays for most of their costs.

The application process for financial aid is usually linked to the Free Application for Federal Student Aid (FAFSA). This is used for public financial aid. If you pursue private financial aid, there are usually individual and specific applications. To apply for all the opportunities that you qualify for, work with your institution's financial aid office.

If you are offered and accept financial aid, it may be paid directly to your institution, or issued to you in one lump sum, or multiple payments throughout the year. There are some scholarships that are based on academic performance, and those will be paid out in installments after each check-in period. When you receive funding, be clear about which financial aid is considered a gift and you do not need to pay back (e.g., a scholarship) and which is considered a loan, which you do need to pay back.

Student loans are a form of financial aid. This is all money that is loaned to you, either through a public or private loan, that you must start paying back upon graduation with added interest. Public student loans usually have lower interest rates and are often based on the income of you and your family. Private student loans are also available but often have higher interest rates.

> **The realities of student loans with Jess: Let's normalize talking about financial aid, student loans, and loan debt. As a student, I didn't learn about the "paying back your loans" part of the process until a few days before my graduation as I sat in a required student loan training. The reality of how much my payments were each month was debilitating, and then I added another student loan on top of it with grad school. My advice to you is that you do the research and design a plan for repayment BEFORE you accept a loan. Be empowered to know the details and take charge. Don't let your student loan payments define your early career. In Chapter 8, we will be discussing money and financial empowerment in depth.**

Other funding opportunities include paid internships, work study, and study grants. If you accept an internship while you are studying, this is an amazing chance to test your skills and knowledge in your field, but they are not always paid. A paid internship will help to offset the transportation costs and your time. When you apply for financial aid, inquire about work-study opportunities. You can often apply for an on-campus job with paid wages, and it could even be within your department or field of study. Lastly, there are unique study grants which a student can receive for a specific scholarly project. It can often include research, study expenses, and travel. These grants may require an end-of-project deliverable. Paid internships, work study, and study grants are all supplementary forms of financial aid.

Your Education Priorities

Regardless of the type of training that you pursue, your education will help you build skills, grow your network, and develop your creative perspective. As you review your training options, remember that it is a personal choice informed by many factors and personal priorities.

Education and training will be a constant in your career, since our field is continuously evolving, and so are we! Plans and interests may also change, which might help you change directions in your education and career plan. Sometimes our education helps to clear up what we do and do not want to pursue, so give time and space for that process.

When you're ready to transition from education to career, it's time for the next step: the job search. In the next chapters, we'll explore how to create dynamic marketing materials and where and how to find jobs.

Figure 3.1 Education Priorities.

Source: Created by Jessica Champagne Hansen using resources from Freepik.com and Macrovector.

Education Priorities

Description

Evaluating your priorities can make decision-making easier. Since education and training are ongoing, you can continue to use this method to help you choose your next step in professional learning and growth.

Circle your priority or priorities in the categories below. Add in specifics that are not listed to customize your plan.

The types of skills you'd like to learn

- Budgets & Management
- Skill/craft
- Communication
- Design
- Organization

The type of educational experience you want

- Specialized
- General Studies
- Hybrid/Multidisciplinary

Your education goals

- Certificate
- AA Degree
- BA Degree
- Other:
- MFA Degree
- PhD Degree
- Internship

The length of training

- Short-term
- Long-term
- Part-time
- Full-time

Your plan to pay for training

- Scholarships
- Financial Aid
- Student Loans
- Pay per class/semester
- Other:

The best learning environment for you

- In person
- Hybrid
- Online
- Other:

The best learning style for you

- Theory & discussion
- Hands-on & project based

Part II
Tools and Strategies for Navigating Your Career Path

4

Job Searching and Networking

You're in Charge

Here's the good news: As a job-seeker, you have a lot of power. You can create dynamic materials that tell your unique story. You can seek out new professional connections, strengthen relationships with people who already know your work, and even create opportunities to showcase your talent.

Here's the not-so-great news: in our industry, the usual job-seeking stuff – browsing online job boards, emailing resumes to HR departments – can be ineffective. The majority of freelance opportunities are never posted publicly and are often filled through phone calls or personal referrals.

Building your professional reputation and network will help you raise your profile in the industry so you can start to tap into the many jobs that never show up on a job board. How do you become the person who gets the call when there's a job that needs to be done? How do you build your professional reputation and network so each job you take leads to the next two opportunities? Let's dive in.

DOI: 10.4324/9781003052227-7

How Do You Decide What to Apply For?

Before you apply for anything, spend some time thinking about what you're looking for right now, at this moment in your career. Here are three questions to ask yourself before you start seeking employment:

- **What opportunities will help you move your career forward?** Applying for *everything* is radically less effective than focusing on specific opportunities that genuinely interest you. You'll make a stronger case for yourself when you understand why you want a job or gig, and how it supports your long-term goals.
- **How much money do you need to make right now, from this area of your employment?** Many of us pay our bills through a combination of income sources. You might be earning your primary income from a "day job," and looking for creative gigs to build your portfolio. In that case, pay rates may be less important than elements like collaborators, creativity, or passion. If you're planning on paying your bills from this work, it's important to know your finances well enough to understand what would make you walk away from a job offer. (We'll talk much more about finances in later chapters!)
- Do you want to work for a larger organization or company, where your job will be more focused? Or do you like working for a smaller, scrappier operation, where you'll have a broader range of tasks? Another way to put this: **do you like being a specialist or a generalist?**

Let's Talk About Specialists vs. Generalists

Some of us like to be a part of a large team or company where we can focus on one piece of a greater whole and enjoy stability and more regularity. Others prefer a more dynamic, smaller group, where they can use a broader range of skills and often exercise more autonomy.

Costume Designer and Technician Dianne K. Graebner loves working in both settings. She says,

> The main distinction between being a specialist for a large company and a generalist for small companies is the difference between

> *security* and *variety*. Like most people, I have had different priorities at different points in my life, and have made decisions with those in mind. Personally, I have always needed the variety. Even while working for a large company full-time, I designed shows at other theaters when possible.

Dianne notes that there may be differences in the amount of support and resources she is given, depending on the size of the theater or production studio:

> The small-budget shows where I have needed to find/build everything can be exhausting, but exciting – especially when I've been the first designer to touch the script. This allows for more creativity but is also a lot more work and there is almost never enough money.

Conversely, projects at larger theaters can give you more time and resources but often come with less freedom to make creative choices. There are also differences in the way you are paid, and your relationship to your employer. Dianne says, "A full-time position at a large company comes with some obvious perks: a regular paycheck, set hours, and often benefits, which are usually not the case with freelance design work."

Ultimately, for Dianne, it's about cultivating her creative portfolio to utilize *all* of her skills:

> Many full-time positions are in technology, as opposed to design. I need to channel my creativity and experience the broad spectrum of environments, people and experiences that come with freelance. It all boils down to one's comfort zone: freelance can be exciting and also stressful, and a full-time position can be comfortable, but you might feel restless. The beauty of developing many skills along the way is that you have more options to create new paths to follow.

Which one appeals to you: being a generalist or a specialist? Or would you, like Dianne, prefer a mix of security and variety? If so, think about how you might balance a more regular and stable job with creative gigs. This "career curation" can impact the kind of job opportunities you pursue.

Job Search Basics

Once you've spent time thinking about the type of job or gig you're looking for, it's time to dive into research. Every area has a unique creative community with its own systems for networking, sharing job opportunities, and communicating. If you're transitioning out of a college or university setting into the professional world, it's important to spend time getting to know the geographic area(s) where you want to work. This can help guide you toward job opportunities and understand how you might fit in.

Let's talk about online job boards. There are dozens of national options and most metropolitan areas will have at least one local job website. Most require employers to post payment information, location, and a description of the job or opportunity. Many will allow you to set up a job-seeker profile where you can save searches, indicate you're looking for work, and even get notifications when certain types of jobs are posted. The majority of job boards now require payment and benefits to be clearly listed on all job postings.

We've shared a few nationwide options below, but encourage you to look for your local and state options as well. All of these options were available at the time of publication of this book, but URLs and website names can change. Some options require paid membership, while others are free for job-seekers.

National arts job boards include:
ArtSearch from Theatre Communications Group (ArtSearch.tcg.org)
Backstage.com
OffstageJobs.com
Art Jobs (Artjobs.artsearch.us)
Playbill jobs board (Playbill.com/jobs)
USITT jobs board (USITT.org/jobs)

Other job websites that often post arts opportunities:
SimplyHired.com
Mandy.com
Indeed.com
FlexJobs.com

Websites focused on teaching jobs:
HigherEdJobs
Edjoin.org
Association of Arts Administration Educators

Not finding much in your industry? Try varying the keywords you use. If you're solely searching for "Costume Designer," you could miss out on a lot of cool gigs that are applicable to your skills but don't use those exact words. Try combinations of keywords: design, tailor, stitching, costumes, wardrobe, and so on.

Part of the benefit of a job search is discovering new opportunities for career pathways where you can use your skillset. How many jobs in your immediate field can you name? Five? Ten? The more research you do and the further you move into your career, the more your awareness of the true range of possibilities in your field will likely expand. This is particularly true if your experience is primarily in an educational setting, like a college theater department. Instead of perhaps 10 or 15 people working as designers and technicians on a university mainstage show, a regional theater may have a team of 50 or 60 artists and artisans working on it, with perhaps dozens more on the arts management and production side.

It's also important to remember that job titles are not standardized. An Assistant Lighting Designer hired as a freelancer for mid-sized production company and an Assistant Lighting Designer on staff at a regional theater may have overlapping duties, but very different payment structures, relationships to other artists, and degree of autonomy and creativity in their work.

Stay open about the types of positions available and don't limit yourself to jobs with a specific title too early in your career. Instead, follow your curiosity and think about the learning and growth opportunities that appeal to you.

More Places to Research

While it's tempting to sit at your computer refreshing these job pages, that's only one piece of the puzzle. When it comes to creative gigs and opportunities in design and tech, *the majority are never posted on those sites – or never posted at all.* Instead, people share information about opportunities through personal connections, networking platforms like Facebook and LinkedIn, alumni groups, and employer websites.

Not sure where to start? Here are a few research areas and action items:

- **Major employers.** What are the theaters, theme parks, rental houses, studios, shops, etc. in your area? Which ones stand out as places you'd like to work? Check out their websites and LinkedIn pages; do you know anyone currently working there? If so, can you reach out to them to talk about their experience and how they got the job?
- **Local awards.** Most cities have at least one annual awards program for live theater, as well as one for independent film. Looking up recent award recipients can help you understand who is working in your field. If you're a sound designer, which sound designers are consistently nominated? Can you look at their websites and see what companies are listed on their resumes? Can you reach out to them and ask if they'd chat with you about their career path?
- **Social media groups and listservs.** Many markets have one or more highly active, moderated Facebook groups or listservs dedicated to networking and sharing job opportunities. There may also be community hashtags you can use to find information, like #LAThtr in Los Angeles. Try looking up "[Your City Name] arts listserv" or "[Your City Name] arts job group" to start.
- **Dedicated networking groups.** Some cities have dedicated networking spaces for the creative sector, such as the Emerging Arts Leaders Networks in many major metropolitan areas.
- **Alumni groups.** Does your school have a local alumni organization? What about a specialized group just for those in the creative industries? Even small colleges and universities may have highly active alumni circles where jobs and opportunities are shared. Seek these out and introduce yourself to the network.

We asked Set Decorator, Prop and Costume Designer Meagan Miller-McKeever to talk about how she's approached networking. Meagan, who attended a small college in southern California, found the networking power of her school's alumni community:

> I've had fellow alumni host me in unfamiliar cities, offer internships, and help negotiate tricky workplace situations. A few years ago,

> I was lucky enough to be part of a 'Women in Film' alumni panel. The speakers were incredibly impressive, mostly show runners and producers from Hollywood and New York. A year later, I was working backstage as a prop woman on a high-profile, primetime show. There was a very uncomfortable situation that I couldn't go to my supervisor about. I reached out to one of the producers from the panel via email, and asked for her advice. She replied in less than two hours with clear, sound guidance. I followed her recommendations and was able to transfer out of that group of co-workers, and then later onto another show that was a better fit for me.

Your network can help you navigate difficult situations and provide advice when you feel stuck.

Whether it's your alumni network or another industry group, spend time cultivating relationships with your peers. Those connections are not only helpful, but they also lead to friendships and jobs! What's Meagan's advice for getting involved with a support network? Be proactive:

> Volunteer at events, introduce yourself on the Facebook or LinkedIn page, and reach out to your fellow community members to offer support. Celebrate the successes of your college community and they will become one of your most important networks for finding your path in the performing arts.

Develop Authentic Networking Strategies (Even If You're an Introvert)

If the word "networking" makes you picture a giant room filled with people dressed in suits, shaking hands, and exchanging business cards, don't worry: it doesn't have to be that way. Networking is usually informal and doesn't have to be intimidating – even if you consider yourself an introvert.

What's the easiest way to network? Lead with curiosity.

Curiosity flips the idea of "networking" from a chore to an opportunity to connect with people doing work you admire. Whether you're browsing someone's website or listening to a conference session, pay attention to what piques your interest. Think about what else you'd like to know about the topic or the person and find opportunities to follow up and learn more. (Flip to the end of the chapter to check out our Networking through Curiosity tool!)

> **Note from Camille the Introvert: I realized early on that I was much more comfortable in networking situations if I was *the one holding the clipboard*. Just attending a conference was intimidating, but volunteering to check people in at the conference gave me a structured way of meeting people. Ushering or working the bar at a theater not only let me see shows for free but also gave me an activity so I could avoid awkwardly standing around! Finding ways to be the one holding the clipboard takes a lot of the pressure off in networking situations – and also demonstrates your work ethic and reliability.**

As for that huge room with hundreds of people? It's not a necessary part of networking, unless you love the energy and excitement of meetings lots of people at once. Think about where you feel the most comfortable and energized: in large groups, small groups, or one-on-one. You can cultivate opportunities for connection in situations where you are most likely to thrive.

Here are a few key strategies for building authentic networks, regardless of whether you identify as an introvert, an extrovert, or somewhere in between.

Informational Interviews

Informational interviews are one of the most powerful tools for a job-seeker and are a great way to build your professional network. An informational interview is an opportunity to ask someone questions about their career and/or the place they work. We like to think of these as "asking cool people to get coffee with you." They often lead to job offers, either in the short-term or long-term.

It is important to note that they are not pitch meetings or opportunities to promote yourself; **you** are interviewing **them.** However, at some point in nearly every informational interview, the conversation will turn to you and the person you're talking to will start to ask you questions. Ideally, you will come out of the interview with a new contact who's invested in your career, and a list of a few additional leads to contact.

How do you decide whom to approach for an informational interview? This is another place to lead with your curiosity ... after you do your research, of course. Who might be able to answer the questions you have about how to build your dream career? Maybe it's that sound designer who keeps getting nominated at local theaters. Maybe it's an alumnus of your college or university who's working for your dream production company. Maybe it's the Technical Director whose resume looks the way you want your own to look in 15 years.

When you're ready to reach out, find their contact information on their website, through professional networking sites like LinkedIn, or by identifying a mutual friend or collaborator to connect you. When you contact them, be as specific as possible and show that you've researched them and are not just doing a school assignment or checking a box. Many professionals receive a lot of these generic outreach emails. It's easy to skip over something if it doesn't feel authentic or specific.

Less successful outreach introduction: "Hi, I'd like to meet with you to talk about Technical Direction. I'm a student."

More successful outreach introduction: "Hello [Name,] I'd love to ask you some questions about your work at Lionsgate, and am curious about how you got involved in USITT's conference planning committee. As a fellow graduate from Southern Oregon University, I would love the opportunity to connect with you and learn more about your path. Would you be willing to do a 30-minute phone call in the next couple of weeks?"

This second email shows the sender's research, their genuine interest, and provides connection points. Their curiosity shines through! It also specifies a time commitment (30 minutes via phone) and suggests a time frame (within the next two weeks). This email is much more likely to get an enthusiastic response than the first, which lacks clarity or specificity.

If you don't hear back within two weeks, follow up respectfully; if you still don't hear anything, move on to a different person. Not everyone will say yes, and that's okay!

Once someone agrees to meet with you, here are some best practices to follow as you're setting up and engaging in an informational interview:

- Suggest a few potential times and dates, and keep an initial meeting to an hour at most. In-person meetings can make it easier to connect with someone, but you should be willing to come to their place of work or neighborhood, or agree to a phone call or virtual meeting.
- Research the person extensively and come to the meeting prepared. You should not ask them any questions that could be answered through a Google search. Instead, questions should demonstrate your research, and engage the person in a deeper discussion.
    - **Inappropriate (Googleable) question**: Does your theater have an internship program?
    - **Appropriate question**: I saw that you worked at Oregon Shakespeare Festival a few years back as an Assistant Director. I've wanted to work there for years. What was that experience like?
- Take notes, visibly. The person you're interviewing will likely suggest resources, more people to contact, and other places to research. Make sure you are valuing their time by writing this great information down!
- Have your resume ready. Remember, this is a conversation about them – but you should also be ready to talk about your own career goals and creative practice. It is appropriate to ask them to review your resume and provide you with feedback.
- Tell them what you're looking for. At the end of the conversation, say something like, "Thank you for meeting with me. I'm actively looking for jobs in ____, at a place like ____. If you see anything, will you send it my way?" This will help them remember to share that juicy job as it comes across their desk. Remember, referrals are a very common way to find work!
- Follow up with an immediate thank you and reiterate your next steps and career goals. You can send a thank-you email or hard-copy card.
- Feel free to reach back out in subsequent weeks or months, especially if you've acted on any of their suggestions for other people to meet with or things to research. This shows that you valued their time and expertise.

You never know when a connection will lead to your next big career move. Sometimes an informational interview generates immediate work, but it can also plant a seed that grows over the course of months or years.

Traditional Networking Spaces

Conferences, workshops, and events are all great opportunities to build your personal network. Some may be specifically dedicated to networking, while others focus on new technology, advocacy, or other major topics in your field. These can be rewarding learning spaces and often provide opportunities to have fun and be social with your peers.

All fields and focus areas have at least one national, professional conference. It's usually annual and often moves from city to city each year. Examples in entertainment technology include the United States Institute for Theatre Technology (USITT) annual conference, which caters to professionals in production and design in live entertainment, or the Kennedy Center American College Theatre Festival for those who are active in their college or university theater departments.

Conferences can be expensive, but there are usually scholarships, student discounts, and opportunities to volunteer for the conference in exchange for free or reduced-price registration (introvert opportunity alert!).

Business Cards

Yes, you still need a business card. You can design and order them online using sites like Moo or Vistaprint, even with little to no graphic design experience, and for less than $25.

All business cards need:

- ◆ **Your name**
- ◆ **A way to contact you quickly and directly (phone or email)**
- ◆ **Enough information about what you do for someone to remember you and reach out (Lighting Designer, Creative Producer, etc.)**

You also might include:

- ◆ **Your website or portfolio URL or QR code**
- ◆ **One image of your work and/or your logo**
- ◆ **Your photo**

Once you're there, identify and attend sessions based on your interests. After a session you really enjoy, introduce yourself to the speakers or panelists. You can start by telling them why you liked the session and asking a follow-up question to engage them in conversation. They will likely ask about your work too. If you feel like you'd like to stay in contact, you can ask them for their business card and/or provide yours.

Before you offer or request a business card, ask yourself: Do I actually need or want to connect with this person? If you request a business card, write a note on the card as soon as possible to help you remember why you want to follow up with them: "Ask about Wolftrap internship experience" or "Worked with Arena Stage TDs, ask about hiring opportunities." Commit to actually following up – and remember, you don't need to exchange cards with everyone!

Mixers, parties, and other big, informal gatherings at conferences provide opportunities to find speakers or presenters and connect with them one-on-one. However, if you do not enjoy these events or find them stressful, look for other casual networking options. Some conferences host "dine-arounds" or other small-group gatherings, and you can often find a more relaxed gathering happening in the conference's hotel lobby or lounge.

Feeding Your Network

Every gig, job, production, or college course you take adds to your network. Like a friendship, though, your networking relationships must be maintained, or they'll start to fade. Here are five tips to help you feed your network:

- ◆ Choose a system for tracking your contacts. LinkedIn is a social network designed for this purpose and has become the standard online networking tool. You may find value in using other social networks, such as Instagram, to find additional ways to connect with your network. Some people still prefer a tangible file, like a business card drawer!
- ◆ Identify the "superconnectors" who seem to know everyone in your field. Often, they are master networkers and can be great people to stay in close contact with.

- Try to reach out to your connections regularly. You can set a calendar reminder to challenge you to reach out to a different connection each week to say hello, share news, and ask how they're doing.
- Share your successes! Don't only reach out when you need help: your network is also there to cheer you on. If you have a new job or a project you're proud of, make sure your network knows. If it's appropriate, add a thank you for their role in your success.
- Celebrate their successes, too! Make it a habit to congratulate people when you see they've done something exciting.

Find a way to connect with others in a way that feels authentic to you and focus on maintaining the professional relationships that feel inspiring and mutually beneficial. Remember, not all connections lead to professional relationships, just like not all conversations lead to friendship! Keep following your curiosity, and you will start to build a network of like-minded artists who inspire you to do your best work.

Self-Producing and Entrepreneurship

The most proactive way to find work? Create it. Many emerging theater professionals turn to self-producing projects, large or small, to build their resume and increase their visibility. Others find innovative ways to leverage their skillsets to create alternative income streams.

While this might feel daunting, know that there are many approaches to creating your own work, ranging from self-producing a full-length script to starting an Etsy site or teaching a workshop on a topic you enjoy. The most successful projects will be the ones grown from your passion for your art form, instead of solely a desire to expand your resume.

Ask yourself:

- **What do I feel pulled to create?**
- **What story do I need to tell?**
- **What is a medium that supports that creation or story?** (Examples: live theater, streaming music, and visual art.)
- **How can I control that medium? What do I need to do to get their story and creation to the public?** (Examples: create a

website, self-produce a short play, and start a new social media account.)
- **Am I excited about creating this opportunity?** If not, pause: this should come from both a desire to tell your story *and* genuine interest in the process of sharing and promoting it.

While you read the following stories from two theater artists/entrepreneurs, think about what you feel drawn to create, teach, or sell, and where you might share or promote it.

Writer and composer Howard Ho found success – and financial gain – as a YouTube creator.

Howard started by doing piano covers featuring his original arrangements, including a *Hamilton* cover in one uninterrupted take. Unsatisfied with the views he was getting, he re-grouped and tried a tutorial: "Since there was still no official sheet music, any pianist who wanted to learn *Hamilton* would inevitably end up watching my video. I released that tutorial, and it did slightly better. I was getting warmer."

However, it wasn't until he tapped into his music history background that he went viral. He shares,

> My Eureka moment came when I realized I could go even further than tutorials. I could explain to people what the notes actually meant and why they added up to an engaging show and soundtrack. Now, many years later, my YouTube series How Hamilton Works has over a dozen videos, 50,000 plus subscribers, millions of views, and most importantly, the Twitter seal of approval from Lin-Manuel Miranda himself.

Howard's success was the result of a clever combination of creativity, musical theater knowledge, and careful study of YouTube's algorithm and feedback. Now, he's using that platform to advance his theater career:

> For the past decade, I've been a sound designer steadily working on shows through word of mouth in the Los Angeles community. When the COVID-19 pandemic shut down live theater, my YouTube channel became my full-time self-employment. Moving forward, I can take that online success and use it to fuel my real-world career, which is now writing my own original musicals.

Similarly, Director Diana Wyenn leveraged her producing and acting skills to jumpstart her career. When she returned home to Los Angeles after studying directing at New York University, she was frustrated by the lack of opportunities to direct. She found it easier to find work as an actor and producer but always made sure to tell people her true passion was directing. Her self-advocacy paid off:

> Soon, playwrights and solo-performers began approaching me with scripts and concepts. They weren't handing me a production or a budget, but these were opportunities to direct. So, I began self-producing and directing projects that aligned with my interests and politics, and had the potential to empower audiences and positively impact communities.

In 2017, she decided it was time to tell a very personal story:

> I read a staggering statistic about the growing global diabetes crisis and decided the most important story I could tell was my own as a Type 1 Diabetic. As I had many times before, I pulled together a team of collaborators I trusted and loved working with, invested my own money to pay them, and got to work. The resulting show, *Blood/Sugar*, has now been seen by thousands, won several awards, and most importantly is dispelling the harmful lies, stigmas, and assumptions surrounding this chronic illness.

It's also become what she sees as her "calling card," showcasing her directorial style and technique.

Although she says she didn't explicitly set out to advance her directing career by self-producing, *Blood/Sugar* has opened new doors for her. She says, "I consistently get approached by other artists, writers, and theater companies who also recognize the power and potential for using theater to advocate for public health, disability and environmental justice, and equity." Her advice to others called to self-produce is "it won't be easy, but it will be rewarding." Diana reflects that self-producing provides an opportunity to

> Work on your skills and technique, establish your style, grow your network of collaborators, become creative and savvy with how you invest both time and money, showcase the kinds of stories

you want to tell and how, and attract future collaborators and employers.

Think about the "companion skills" you have alongside your design and technical skillset. Are you a strong writer? Do you enjoy social media? Do you like to create your own projects? There's no limit to your creativity and no rules for how you advance your career. If you feel called to create and express yourself, do it!

Be Brave. Be Authentic. Be Yourself.

Just like every artist is unique, every creative career pathway will look different. Your approach to seeking and securing jobs should reflect your values, personality, and needs. Some people enjoy the stability of working full-time for a large organization and may seek jobs in a more traditional way, by applying directly to the organization with a cover letter and resume. Others may prefer a portfolio career made of many gigs and part-time opportunities and will need to rely more on networking, personal promotion, and entrepreneurship.

After you've done the research, dive into your local arts community. You don't need to wait to be hired to become a part of the creative culture. Read interviews with local artists. Seek out and attend free creative events, such as advocacy days or work-in-progress readings. If you're on a tight budget, volunteer to usher or reach out to arts organizations to ask about free or reduced-price ticket options. You will start to develop knowledge of the local community, and, most importantly, hone your artistic taste and identify potential creative collaborators.

Regardless of your career goals, we hope this chapter has given you proactive tools to support your job search. Next, we'll dive into how to create personalized marketing materials that showcase your individuality and talent.

Job Searching and Networking ♦ 71

Figure 4.1 Networking through Curiosity.

Source: Created by Camille Schenkkan and Jessica Champagne Hansen using resources from Freepik.com and Macrovector.

Networking Through Curiosity

Description

Use the template below to consider how you'll expand your network in a way that feels authentic and connects you to people you admire. Answer the questions below to find the intersection of networking and curiosity.

WHO

- Who is doing work you admire?
- What do you like about it?
- What questions might you ask them about it?
- How and when might you approach this person or these people?

WHERE

- Where do you want to work?
- What do you want to know about working there?
- Do you know anyone who works there? If so, how will you find someone and ask them for an informational interview?

Networking Curiosity

WHY

- What excites you about your work and why do you do it?
- What do you feel are your professional and creative strengths?

WHAT

- What do you want to learn, experience or know?
- Where might you study, experience, ask about, or observe these things?

Follow Up

Commit to taking one action listed above per month. Hint: You can include networking goals in the career plans you'll create later in the book!

Figure 4.2 Job Profile.

Source: Created by Jessica Champagne Hansen using resources from Freepik.com and Macrovector.

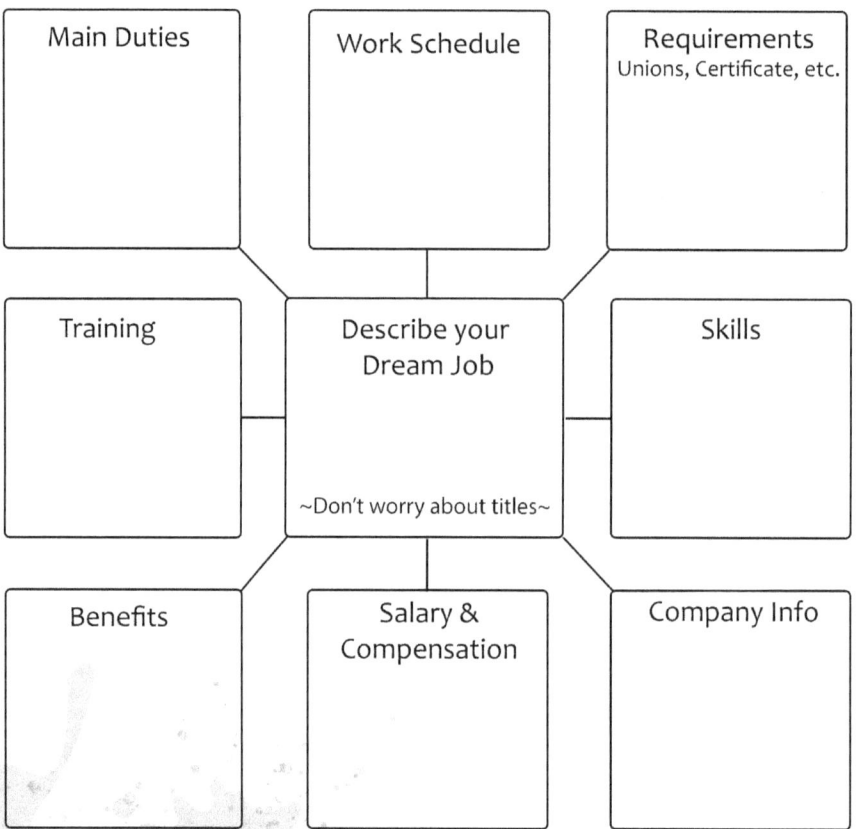

5

Career Marketing Materials

Career Marketing Materials Overview

The materials you create to market yourself need to tell your story: who you are, what you do, how you do it, and what you see as the next step in your career. Luckily, creative individuals are storytellers! We can use our resumes, cover letters, and other documents to not only outline our hard and soft skills but also to showcase our creativity.

This chapter will cover resumes and curricula vitae (CV), cover letters, portfolios, and personal websites and use of social media. We'll also share best practices for submitting your materials when you're ready to apply for a job or gig.

Note that this information was written for job opportunities within the United States. Conventions and best practices can differ greatly in other countries; for example, in some countries it is common to see the marital status and other personal information on a resume. If you're looking at jobs abroad, be sure to spend time researching job application best practices in that country.

"I have a great portfolio, strong network and sparkling personality so I can skip this chapter"

Sadly, nope. Everyone, regardless of their professional goals, will need to create a resume and cover letter at some point in their career. Most of us will actually need multiple resumes, each highlighting different aspects

DOI: 10.4324/9781003052227-8

of our professional skills. Many creative individuals will also need a website, portfolio, or both. Use of social media is a personal choice but can support career development.

It's also true that you will likely be offered a job or gig solely through personal recommendation or networking, with no resume or other documents required. As you progress further in your career, that will probably happen more frequently as you build a reputation and make more professional connections.

For now, read through the information below, even if you aren't sure when you'll need these application tools. We highly recommend starting them *before* you need them, though, as job applications have quick turnaround times and these materials take time to develop.

Aesthetic and Personal Brand

While your marketing materials should be professional and easy to read, they also need to reflect your personality and the art you make and love. The visual component of this is sometimes called your *aesthetic*. The combination of your aesthetic, the art you make, your personality, and your work style create your *personal brand*.

Choose two or three artists or creative professionals whose work you admire and spend a few minutes exploring their website or social media. Notice the visual components, the words they use, and the way it makes you feel. Does their online presence reflect their creative work? Can you determine anything about their values or personality?

Thinking about your personal brand can bring up some big questions. Who are you as an artist? What kind of creative work do you love? If you are a designer, what is your signature style? If you're a technician, stage manager, or other creative professional, what adjectives describe your work style and personality? (For support around answering these questions, check out the exercises in Chapter 10!)

We asked arts educator and digital marketer Courtney Clark to tell us a little about their personal brand and how it shows up in their online presence. Courtney shared,

> My personal brand is **fun**, **creative**, and **honest**. Instead of seeing social media and my online presence as 'marketing myself,' I see it

as a space reflective of my truth, creativity, and experiences (both professionally *and* personally). This allows me to connect with others in an authentic and genuine manner through the digital space.

Courtney's self-knowledge shines through in their website and social media, both of which reflect not only their professional skillset but also their personal values.

Finding Your Personal Brand
How do you like to work? What do you bring to a team? Do you thrive in highly structured or hierarchical environments, or do you crave a more casual, collaborative workplace? All of these questions can help you tap into your personal brand. Think about how you might describe yourself in a professional setting, and how past colleagues and collaborators might describe you.

Circle three words or phrases below that reflect what you bring to a creative, professional environment. Feel free to add additional choices in the margin, particularly around areas of your identity that you feel are essential parts of your personal brand; examples might be "Latinx heritage," "nonbinary gender identity," or "neurodiversity."

Humor	Teaching/Education
Professionalism	Strategy
Anti-Racist Practice	Inclusivity
Fresh Perspective	Communication
Power-Sharing	Activism
Play	Fun
Organizational Skills	Collaboration
Integrity	Focus
Mentorship	Innovation
Disruption of Status Quo	Ingenuity and Problem-Solving
Efficiency/Speed	LGBTQ+ Perspective
Leadership	Cultural Perspective

Your personal brand reflects your values, your background, and how you "show up" in a professional setting. It's often what people remember about you, even more than your design or technical skills. Knowing your personal brand can help you seek out environments that support all aspects of your identity and uplift your values.

Finding Your Aesthetic
Which words would you use to describe your visual aesthetic? Here are a few ideas. If you're a designer, these could be reflected in your creative work. If you're a technician, manager, or other creative professional, they might be the type of design you're drawn to or enjoy. You might get clues by looking around your workspace or thinking about the art you love.

Circle the top three that resonate with you, or add your own in the margin. Think about how your application materials might reflect these through design elements, fonts, color, layout, or imagery.

Whimsical	Harmonious
Dynamic	Earthy
Strong	Fragmented
Abstract	Bold
Beautiful	Geometric
Ethereal	Warm
Explosive	Industrial
Provocative	Surreal
Sensual	Inviting
Playful	Delicate
Organic	Vibrant
Fluid	Minimalist
Elegant	Serene
Stimulating	

You can express your aesthetic in the fonts you choose, the layout of your materials, the color palette on your website, and the images you select. For example, a resume, cover letter, and portfolio submitted for a design gig should all have consistent fonts and design elements. Think about repeating elements, like a consistent header with your name and contact information, or a monogram that appears on your resume, website, and social media profile image.

If you are a visual artist, you may want to design your materials yourself. If you aren't, there are many free and highly affordable template options available online – just search for "creative resume and cover letter templates." Once you find one you like, you will need to think critically about whether to keep, delete, or modify the sections they suggest; don't feel you need to follow their recommendations exactly. Remember that whatever template you choose should reflect your aesthetic, while still being easy to read.

All of your materials should work together to tell a consistent story about you as a creative professional, from the visual aesthetic to the words you use to describe yourself. Courtney Clark tells us,

> My branding represents my values while demonstrating my artistic aesthetic. My use of organic shapes, colorful vintage scenes, and installation-based art all work in tandem with my voice as I share content and speak on my experiences with mental health and wellness and as a queer person.

Their design choices reinforce the way they speak, act, and the layers of identity they bring into any workplace.

Sit with the words you circled from the lists above and start imagining how they might influence the way your marketing materials look and feel. What is the story you're telling?

Resumes

The most common and widely used personal marketing document is a resume. A resume is a brief, focused overview of an individual's work experience, education, skills, and accomplishments.

Nearly everyone reading this book will need to create multiple resumes, one for each specialization. If you are both a designer and a technician, you'll need separate resumes for each of those skillsets. For example, one professional might have a costume design resume, a costume technician resume, a lighting design resume, and a teaching resume, each highlighting different gigs and skillsets. Early in their career, that same individual might also have a service industry resume outlining their "day job" work.

Why can't you just send a prospective employer *all* of the information, and let them see your full range of experience? While you might think more information is better, employers will spend *only a few seconds* initially reviewing your resume to assess your baseline qualifications. This is a lean, mean document that presents information quickly and cleanly.

Specificity is key: the more focused a resume is on the exact requirements of a job or opportunity, the better your chances are of being considered. If you want to let an employer know you have additional skillsets, you can always write "Costume Design and Scenic Painting resumes available upon request" at the bottom. The exception would be a 'hybrid' job, like an in-house Assistant Costume Designer position that requires both strong design acumen and technical skills.

As you progress further in your career, more and more of your early gigs will naturally come off of your resume to make room for others. It is an evolving and ever-changing document that provides a snapshot of your current experience and abilities. Consider keeping a master resume with all of your experience included, which you can then edit depending on the job. You should always go back to storytelling: how does your resume answer the question, "Why am I the best one for this job or opportunity?"

If you're making a career shift or have seemingly unrelated experience, such as a previous career in a different field, you can choose whether to list it or not. Know that employers are often happy to see things like customer service on a resume, as they recognize the value in transferrable skills! You may also choose to highlight seemingly separate jobs to make a case for why you're the best one for a position; an example would be someone applying to teach lighting design with no direct previous experience, but whose resume includes both lighting design gigs and past experiences teaching at a summer camp.

If you are worried about a prospective employer contacting other people you've worked with – especially if you haven't told a current boss you're thinking about leaving – add the words "Applicant requests that job search be kept confidential" at the very bottom of your resume. Employers respect this request.

All resumes need the following elements. They usually appear in the order listed here, although some people choose a less common layout that puts education at the bottom, for example. Feel free to get creative, but make sure people can find the information they need quickly and easily.

Your Full Professional Name and Contact Information
This should include an email address, which is ideally some version of your name (yes, it's time to retire that SparklePony2014@email.com account). It should also include a phone number connected to a working phone with an available voicemail inbox. You can choose whether to include a mailing address or just your city and state. Some people prefer not to share their physical address, for privacy reasons. You may also choose to include your website, portfolio, and/or social media handles in this section; consider hyperlinking them for easy clicking.

Overview of Education and Training
Briefly list your college or university and any degrees attained or in progress. If you are not attending college or university, list your high school diploma or GED. Graduation years are optional and often are excluded by mid-career or seasoned professionals. GPA is also optional, and most employers do not miss it if it isn't included. You may also choose to include training programs or certifications; these can go in this section or farther down, under Skills or in a separate Training section.

Example

Education

- Bachelor of Arts in Theater Arts, Humboldt State University, expected 2025
- Associate of Arts in Theater Arts, College of the Siskiyous, 2022
- Safety in Theater Workplaces Residential Training Program, 2022

Relevant Work Experience
This should be the main part of a resume. The title of the section, or header, varies depending on what your resume is focused on; "Work Experience," "Costume Design Experience," and "Teaching Experience" could all be headers for the work experience section of a creative professional's resume. You can have more than one section if desired – for example, separate sections for Costume Designer and Assistant Costume Designer if you have a few credits in each area. Remember

that internships, fellowships, time at summer stock, and other training program opportunities can absolutely be included in the work experience portion of your resume.

The way you list your experience varies, depending on whether it was a job or long-term gig, or if you are listing experience working on a specific production or project.

For a job: Write the job title, the organization or company, the time you spent working there (listed as months or years), and then no more than five short sentences describing your primary duties. Those are often formatted as bullet points and should relate directly to the job you're applying for. Connect the dots for the employer! Usually, this section is in reverse chronological order, with the most recent experience first.

Example
Assistant Lighting Designer, Modern Theater; Jan. 2021–Feb. 2022

- Worked directly with visiting designers to realize their vision and stay on-budget and on-time
- Responsible for inventory of 250+ instruments, handling all supply orders and equipment maintenance
- Principal designer for all second-stage, educational, and work-in-progress projects
- Led a team of four part-time design assistants and interns

For design or tech work on a production or project: If you had multiple gigs with the same job title, create a section for that title. Under it, write the production/project and author/playwright, key artists (often the director), theater or production company, and year.

Example
Assistant Costume Designer

In the Blood (Suzan-Lori Parks), Dir. Tina Patel	Nueva Voices Theatre, 2020
A Doll's House (Ibsen), Dir. Maria Ilog	Nueva Voices Theatre, 2019
Mojada (Luis Alfaro), Dir. Ben Reyes	Glendale College Theatre, 2018

Always remember that honesty is key. If a project took place through college theater that should be clear on your resume. Never try to make a project, role, or position sound different than it was.

Skills

This is a key section for creative professionals. If a job posting calls out specific skills as necessities, make sure they're included in your resume when you apply. If relevant, you can indicate your level of proficiency: beginner, intermediate, advanced, and expert are standard terms to use.

The skills section is primarily for "hard skills," which are abilities, training, or knowledge that you need to do a specific job. "Soft skills," also called interpersonal skills, are best demonstrated through your work experience section; for example, you can highlight "communication skills" or "collaboration" in a bullet point about a previous job. This context is more helpful than solely listing these attributes in a Skills section.

It should go without saying that you should not list a skill that you don't actually have. You can always list your current level, using words like beginner, intermediate, or advanced.

Your skills section may include:

- Computer programs or software, such as AutoCAD or Q Lab
- Specific technical skills, such as Tailoring, Scenic Painting, or Automation Programming
- A limited number of soft skills relevant to the job you hope to have, such as Team Management, Conflict Resolution, or Written & Verbal Communication. Use these sparingly and make sure they are specific and relevant (see "Beware the Fluff")!

Example

Skills: Stitching; tailoring; flat pattern drafting; dyeing; shopping; AutoCAD (intermediate); Microsoft Office Suite (intermediate); leadership of teams of 10+ individuals

Other Sections

You may also choose to include one or more of the following sections or create your own to call out particular areas of interest or experience.

Just remember to keep it focused and relevant to the position you're seeking.

- Awards and recognition: Examples might include Kennedy Center American College Theater Festival honors, scholarships, or academic recognition such as Phi Beta Kappa.
- Certifications and licenses: Examples might include OSHA 10 or 30-hour training certification, a Class B driver's license, or American Red Cross Lifeguard Certification.
- Union status: If you are a member of a union related to the job you're seeking, be sure it is listed on your resume. If there are different tiers or status levels in your union, include that information as well.
- Other memberships or organizational affiliation: This could include membership to a service organization (Individual Member, Americans for the Arts), a networking organization (Executive Committee, Emerging Theater Leaders Houston), or an artistic group (Artistic Collaborator, Pennsylvania Theater Co.).

If you only have one item in these areas (e.g., a Class B driver's license but no other certifications or licenses), we recommend including it in another section, such as Skills. You might need to rename the section – for example, switching Skills to Skills & Certifications.

> **Beware the Fluff.** Almost everyone has "fluff" in their resume that doesn't actually provide valuable information to prospective employers. This includes Overview or About Me sections, which often say something vague like "My goal is to find a valuable place to make a meaningful contribution," or overuse of the Skills section, where people sometimes list descriptions like collaborative, good communicator, or team player. Look critically at these sections: Are the words you're using too vague? Can you be more specific – or delete them to make room for other sections?

References: Your Personal Cheerleaders

You can choose whether to include a References section on your resume or to add "References Available Upon Request" at the bottom. Check the job posting to see whether they require references and, if so, if there is a set number they want you to include.

Whether or not you include it on your standard resume, your references are a key part of your job search. They are your personal cheerleaders, who can back up everything you say in your marketing materials with personal knowledge and warmth.

We recommend maintaining relationships with at least four prospective references. These should not be people in your family and should all be able to speak to your professional and creative abilities. When you're creating a resume for a job or gig, think about what combination of references would make the strongest case for why you are the best one for the job.

References can be:

- Current or former supervisors. This is a great reference choice, as they have direct knowledge of your professional skillset and work style. For a designer or technician, this might be a producer or director who has hired you in the past.
- Professors or teachers. This is most common for early-career individuals just coming out of an educational setting. Be sure these references understand where you are in your career, *now* – especially if it's been a year or two since they worked with you.
- Colleagues. Sometimes, a creative collaborator or other colleague can provide a strong reference, especially if the job you're seeking is similar to the situation in which you worked with this collaborator.

Before you list someone as a reference, have an honest conversation with them about your career goals and directly ask them if they will provide you with a strong recommendation. This is also the time to double-check their contact information and current job title. If you sense any hesitancy around providing a stellar recommendation, find a different reference!

Above All: Keep It Real

Do not feel like you need to pad your resume if you're very early in your career, or just don't have a lot of relevant experience. Someone who is just starting in their field might only have one or two jobs, internships, or apprenticeships listed – and that is okay, and normal.

What isn't okay: lying or misrepresenting your experience, qualifications, or education. Not only is it morally wrong, it could result in consequences for you, your employer, and your colleagues. Two of the most common resume "fibs" are implying you completed a degree but didn't, and mispresenting your role or job title in a past position; know that degree completion and past employment will all be verified as a part of a standard background check.

If you've worked as an assistant to a designer, you need to make it clear that you're showing images of the work created by the designer, and that you supported that design. Think carefully about whether including a photo of someone else's design could be unintentionally misleading, even if you did work on the production or project. Be sure the role you played on the project is very clear, and that you credit the designer(s) as well.

Curriculum Vitaes

Let's talk about the difference between a resume and a curriculum vitae, or CV. While these terms are sometimes used interchangeably by employers, these are different documents. You may need to read between the lines of a job posting to understand if they truly want a full curriculum vitae or are really asking for a resume.

In the United States, CVs are primarily used in educational settings, such as a hiring process at a college or university. Unlike a resume, a CV is intended to be as comprehensive as possible; they can be 50 pages or more for a seasoned professional.

A CV has all of the information contained in a resume, and also includes the following:

- ◆ A comprehensive list of teaching experience, including courses, workshops, etc., with location and dates included
- ◆ Papers, books, and other publications with topics and dates published

- Speaking appearances and conference presentations
- For designers, dramaturgs, directors, etc., a complete listing of productions and projects
- Other creative projects, collaborations, gallery showings, etc.

If you believe teaching is in your future, start tracking these things now; trying to remember the date of a conference presentation ten years in the past is much harder than jotting notes as you go. If you're not ready to create an actual CV, you can put basic information into a spreadsheet so it's accessible when you do need to submit one.

Cover Letters

Cover letters are often required when you apply to a part-time or full-time job. A cover letter answers the question, **why are you the best candidate for this job or opportunity?** Think of it less as a formality or extra piece of paper, and more as a persuasive essay. This is where you make your case for why your skills, work, and life experience make you uniquely qualified for the job you want.

Brent Bruin, pattern maker and fitter for film, television, and theater, has seen hundreds of cover letters from a variety of technicians and creative professionals. He says,

> A great cover letter takes time, thoughtful planning, and direct application of your experience to the job you are applying for. Specificity is key, as is going back to the basics of solid composition: 1. Tell the reader what you are going to say, 2. Say it clearly, and 3. Summarize what you just said.

It's also where your passion and genuine interest need to shine through. The reader should understand why you'd be excited to work on their project or in their shop. A great cover letter shares enough of your personality to make the hiring manager want to meet you and learn more.

A cover letter should be formatted like a standard business letter, using what is called block format. There are multiple types of block letter (block, modified block, and semi-block), with slight variations in layout.

You can decide which works best for you. All business letters have the date of the letter, the name and address of the sender, a salutation or greeting, body paragraphs, a closure (like Sincerely), and a signature. If you're unfamiliar with business letter format, find a template online or research block format so you can be confident in the presentation of your materials.

Before you write your cover letter, spend time with the description of the job, opportunity, or gig. Whether that description is just a paragraph or several pages long, it's your job to hone in on what is most important to the person or company making the hire. This gives you information about what to focus on in your cover letter.

Look for:

- What is unique to *this exact job*. Remember: a Costume Assistant at a small production company and a Costume Assistant at a large regional theater may have very different job descriptions. What duties, projects, or responsibilities are listed in the description? What *isn't* listed that you would have assumed would be a part of this job?
- Repeated descriptive words, like "manage," "safety," "friendly," or "collaborative." This gives a sense of the values of the hiring manager or company, and what soft skills they're seeking in an applicant. Think about how your experience reflects each of those traits or values.
- Hard skills or certifications required, such as "carpentry," "AutoCAD proficiency," or "experience with automation." It's essential that you list these in your resume; you can consider expanding on them or mentioning them in your cover letter, too.

If you are applying for a position where you don't have direct experience, you need to address why you're interested in a career shift, and how that shift supports your long-term goals. Employers want someone to not only be able to fulfill job duties but also be happy and fulfilled in their work. If it is a job and not a short-term gig, they are looking for someone whose career trajectory clearly shows demonstrated interest in this work. If your resume doesn't show direct experience, you need to make a case for why you are making a switch.

You also need to research the hiring manager, company, organization, and/or project. If it's a creative gig, think about why you're drawn to the type of art they're making. If it's a company or organization, consider why you want to work *there* instead of at a competitor or different type of company.

Let's look at how someone interested in a Costume Shop Manager job in a university setting might prepare to write their cover letter. Let's pretend this person has experience in costume shops, but no direct experience as an educator, or working in a university setting. First, they look at the job description and make notes on what stands out to them.

Example:

College Costume Shop Manager Job

The primary responsibility of the position is managing the costume shop for the Theater and Dance Programs' performing arts seasons which include four theater pieces, two dance concerts, and smaller productions as needed. Will be responsible for realizing the design of the productions in collaboration with the costume designer, directors, production manager, and students. This may include original designs, reworking stock, rentals, loans, or any combination thereof. The Costume Shop Manager will assume primary responsibility for the overall coordination of the shop work flow and effort to realize the aesthetic, budgetary, and theatrical needs of the production season for the department. Minimum of four years prior professional experience in the field managing productions or a costume shop. Expert in collaboration, pattern-making, draping, some tailoring, craft knowledge, hair & makeup, dyeing, creative problem-solving, and budgeting. Historical aspects of costume, construction methods, fabrics, pattern-making, crafts, wigs, makeup, and design processes. Ensuring students use the equipment properly under supervision. Ability to instruct in the art and techniques of costuming. Use industrial and home sewing machines, serger, embroidery, dye equipment, and millinery equipment. Energy, flexibility, patience, and ability to work with diverse students.

Applicant's annotations:

- ◆ *combo of costume generalist and educator . . . doing and teaching simultaneously*

- broad range of design and technician skills
- many references to management and collaboration
- many projects happening at once!

Next, they develop their strategy. This involves thinking about where they are highly qualified, and where they need to make a case for why they could do the job even if they don't have direct experience or knowledge.

Example

Big things I want to highlight:

- Generalist skills: I have a broad range of skills from working in summer stock and on both contemporary and classical regional theaters.
- Educator skills: Need to make the case that while I haven't worked in an educational setting, I have supervised interns, lead teams with varying skill levels, and have a strong commitment to mentorship.
- Management: Highlight budgeting and project management skills gained in my time in a costume rental shop.

Once you've done this prep work, it's time to answer the big question: how does your unique combination of life experience, work experience, and personality make you the best one for *this unique opportunity, at this company/organization, at this time?* You need to be clear on this or the employer won't be either.

Remember how we encouraged you not to list your soft skills on your resume? Your cover letter is a great place to highlight skills like collaboration, leadership, management, and communication, in the context of past jobs. For example, if you feel like the job needs a strong team manager, you can speak to how you managed a team of ten people in a previous position. If you see a lot of references to communication skills in the job description, you might dedicate a paragraph to how you've developed your communication acumen through your past gigs.

> **Writer's block? If you're finding it hard to start your cover letter or aren't sure what to say, we recommend:**
>
> - **Talking it out with a friend or relative. Tell them about the job, and why your skills and experience make you a great fit. You can even ask them to take notes for you while you talk!**
> - **Do something physical, like walking or swimming, while you think about what you want to say. This can help you organize your thoughts.**
> - **Do a Terrible First Draft. Let yourself free-write a messy, convoluted, definitely-not-block-format, unprofessional, passionate, way-too-casual first draft. Then read it once, delete it, take a break, and start again. It works.**

Let's see an example of a cover letter for that Costume Shop Manager job. The applicant has already done the work of deciding what they want to highlight in their cover letter; now they just need to put it into the right format. We asked Brent to pretend to be this applicant and write an effective cover letter. Check out the next page to see what he created.

Brent skillfully made a case for why he was the best one for the position, despite not having 100% of the desired experience. His letter is clear, concise, and persuasive.

As you can see, a great cover letter takes time, planning, and a solid strategy. Specificity is the key to a successful cover letter! You will have a much better chance at advancing to the interview stage if you do this deep thinking and approach a cover letter as an opportunity to make a case for yourself.

Portfolios

A portfolio is a useful tool for designers and technicians. It may be required for some job applications and is also a helpful tool for sharing your artistry with prospective collaborators and employers. Portfolios use images, words, and even video to showcase your design perspective and technical abilities. After looking at your portfolio, someone should have a clear sense of your aesthetic and what you bring to a creative team.

Figure 5.1 Cover Letter Sample.

Source: Brent Bruin.

Cover Letter Sample

Brent M. Bruin
Email Address · Phone Number

Date

College
2134 West Main Street
Los Angeles, CA 90012

Dear Hiring Manager,

Please accept my application for Costume Shop Manager for the College as seen in an ad on your website. For the past eight years, I have been the Costume Shop Manager at the Regional Theatre in Los Angeles, CA, and hold my M.F.A. in Costume Technology from the University of North Carolina School of the Arts. Over the course of my career, education has been the foundation for professional development, mentorship, and management.

Working in different kinds of theater has broadened my skill set. Earlier in my career in summer stock, the shop supervisor helped me round out and refine my skills. As I moved to other regional theaters, I was ignited by this mindset, and would always ask to take on new types of projects. As a result, I found many transferable skills, which I apply to my dressmaking and tailoring work. This approach has led me to be enthusiastic about uncharted projects and think critically about unknown costuming topics.

I enjoy the learning atmosphere in collaborative costume shops where high-skilled staff mentor and develop junior staff. I take this approach when I manage shops and ignite a spark for learning and development. Fostering the development of emerging artists at a university is very much the same as training interns, supervising teams, and mentoring staff. I take the same approach as my first shop supervisor, learn what the students need, and find ways to nurture their growth.

A costume manager requires the ability to supervise all aspects of large projects. For example, I was a mid-level manager at a costume rental house and oversaw chorus rental packages. I would receive the design, measurements, and budget from the designer or producing organization and would lead a team to pull together a package to be sent out. This work required detailed planning, organization, and budgeting, often with multiple orders having close ship-out dates. As a result, I developed a system for organizing each project and assigned a certain number of days to ensure prompt progress. This system allowed me to analyze current and new deadlines and staff labor needs. In addition, I kept in communication with my team on their daily progress and helped them solve issues that arose.

The Shop Manager position at the College would further my vocational education, my passion for education, and employ my leadership skills to make for a more robust costume professional.

Sincerely,

Brent M. Bruin

Brent M. Bruin

When deciding what to include in your portfolio, think about how you can illustrate your *range*, your *technique*, and your *aesthetic*. Remember that the portfolio itself, not just the content inside, can show that you are organized, pay attention to detail, understand color theory, communicate visually, and more! Think about the look and feel of your portfolio, and how it reinforces who you are as an artist.

Just like with a resume, you will customize your portfolio for each interview. If you are meeting with a team about a new theme park parade, for example, you might move your work in theater for young audiences and musical theater to the front of your portfolio to call out your relevant skills.

Portfolios can be physical books or binders, shareable digital formats such as a PDF, or can be hosted on a website. Each format has advantages, and you will likely have multiple versions of your portfolio ready to utilize in different situations. For example, you might share out a link to your portfolio on your website in an initial job inquiry, send a digital version when you're invited to apply, and then bring a hard-copy version to an in-person interview.

> **If you are looking for an in-depth book on portfolios for technical theater, check out *Show Case* by Rafael Jaen. The information about portfolio formats, layouts, and organization for physical portfolios is complete and thorough. There are also great tips and tricks from industry professionals.**

Physical Book Portfolios

A physical portfolio can be beneficial for in-person interviews, networking events, or "portfolio reviews" conducted by a university or at a hiring event.

If you're working on a physical portfolio, remember that print quality is an important component of the process. The final product must have clean and clear resolution for both the photos and the text on the pages. Be sure to compare the colors from screen to printed product, as they can shift during the process. Print quality is just as important as the resolution of the original files!

There are many options for creating custom portfolio books using online services and templates. Each site offers different size, paper, binding, and cover options. You can choose to print "on demand," creating smaller portfolios by topic or industry to help customize for interviews. Custom portfolio books are great because they are completed, printed, and shipped right to you. The drawback is that you will need to create new books periodically to update your work.

Digital (PDF) Portfolios

Digital portfolios allow you to carry all of your work with you, on a tablet, laptop, or flash drive. There are many online tools for creating a cohesive and professional digital portfolio presentation.

Note that your digital portfolio and your website are not the same thing. You will need a separate digital portfolio that can be easily shared, emailed, and uploaded/downloaded. Many designers and technicians also include their digital portfolio on their website, for anyone to access and download. Conversely, you can link out from your digital portfolio to your website or social media, in case viewers want more information about a project.

One of the best ways to format your digital portfolio is to create a PDF, which can be viewed and navigated on a tablet in a live interview or shared digitally for a virtual interview. Having the actual portfolio file downloaded and ready is helpful when internet access is not reliable in the interview location, and you are able to guide the viewer more easily than if they were just navigating freely on a website. Because it is digital, this style of portfolio is easy to update and customize. You can use Adobe programs (like InDesign or Illustrator) to create a custom file or use templates from PowerPoint, Googleslides, or Canva.

When you're asked to share a digital portfolio, you can send it via large file sharing programs or send a link to where it's hosted online. Once you have your portfolio completed, consider linking to it in your email signature and sharing it out via social media. Be proud of your work and share your accomplishments!

Organization and Best Practices

Organize your portfolio with a beginning, middle, and end. We are storytellers, and our portfolios should have a flow that shows experiences and skills in a cohesive way. Imagine that you are curating a gallery, leading the audience from one set of art to the next.

Portfolios should start with an introductory page. This should have your name, title, and photo(s) of your work that are a sneak peek of your talents. The portfolio cover will probably be face-up during the first few minutes of the interview and a great intro page will get the team excited to see more of your work!

Portfolios are often organized by project, with the project you're most proud of, or which best showcases your skills, coming first. If you're primarily a technician, you may choose to organize your portfolio by skillset (e.g., tailoring, draping, and stitching) instead of by project. A good rule of thumb is no more than five pages per project or skillset, and no more than five projects per portfolio; few people will look through the entire thing, even if they are excited about hiring you.

It is important to show the process for your portfolio projects (not just the final product). This gives the viewer an idea of how you work both creatively and collaboratively. Rough sketches, color swatches, technical drawings, fitting photos, paint tests, and in-process photos illustrate how you work during the preproduction and production phases.

Page Layout
Consider what page layout provides the best opportunity to showcase the work you do, and whether you want to create your portfolio in portrait or landscape format. This can depend on your creative discipline. For example, costume design renderings are usually presented on a portrait layout, and scenery renderings are usually in landscape.

Options for page layouts include:

- Single content: One image and accompanying text/label. This is a great choice for high-quality, standalone images that make a strong statement about your work.
- Multiple content: Two to three images and accompanying text/labels. This can be handy for multiple images from a specific project.
- Collage without overlap: Multiple images and accompanying text/labels, which can vary in size but do not overlap one another. This could be presented in rows, columns, or like a collage with organic composition. This can be useful for showing process, or multiple aspects of a project.
- Collage with overlap: Multiple visuals and text/labels that overlap and can vary in size. Be sure you aren't crowding or confusing the viewer's eye.

♦ Tile/Grid layout: Multiple visuals and text/labels that are presented in a grid like tiles. These could all be the same size or presented in multiple sizes which fit together on the grid.

Whatever layout you choose, and regardless of whether your portfolio is a binder or a PDF, it is helpful for the portfolio to stay consistent in use of landscape or portrait format from beginning to end. The consistency will help viewers appreciate your work, without getting caught up in where to look or turn to next.

Photos
Taking clean, clear, high-resolution photos of your process and final products needs to be a consistent part of your work. If you have a blurry or pixelated photo of your work, it is actually better to not include it at all. This could mean that your best work is missing from your portfolio unless you get great photos. Use a smart phone or hire a colleague to document your work if you don't feel your photography skills or equipment are strong enough. Our work is only as good as the photos that document it.

Labels
Text labels are an essential part of your portfolio. Every project or show should be labeled on the front page with any supporting information to identify the project, that is, the show name, your role, the creative team and theater, show information and concept, and so on. In *Show Case* by Rafael Jaen, he emphasizes the importance of the four C's of labeling in your portfolio: clean, clear, consistent, and correct spelling. The last one cannot be emphasized enough! Be sure to check for spelling and accuracy of text and label information.

Make sure your role on the project is very clear, and if others' work is also shown, credit them. For example, if you were an Assistant Scenic Designer, you need to not only include that information but also credit the Scenic Designer as well. If you did not take a photo, you need to clearly credit the photographer.

Updating and Editing
As you work, you will continue to have more content to add to your online website, digital PDF portfolio, and a physical book style portfolio(s). Keep a file (physical, digital, or both) to store your projects as you are

busy working. Periodically, you will need to update everything and select your new best projects that show your experiences and skills. Every now and then (or more) you may decide to try a new format, layout, style, or branding for your portfolio. This is a full refresh and will take a little more time but shows how you are changing as an artist!

> **Note from Jess the Designer: I suggest updating your portfolio materials at least once a year. Each summer, when I have more time in my schedule, I dedicate a few days to updating my website, digital portfolio and portfolio books, CV, resume, and professional networking sites. Pick a time when your schedule is slower and update your marketing materials. You won't regret it, especially when you get a last-minute call for a great project.**

Whether you're working on your first portfolio or are updating it for the 54th time, it is helpful to have someone else look at it to provide feedback, test your site links, and offer their thoughts on navigation and clarity. They will be able to spot inconsistencies and spelling errors that you missed from staring at it for so long. Ask them if the text descriptions are clear and if they understand what they are looking at. Also, ask them if anything is unnecessary. You only get so much space in your portfolio, and you want each piece to highlight your skills and experience.

Websites

Many designers and technicians create personal websites where they can host their portfolio and resume and share information about current projects. Creating a website can be as simple as setting up an out-of-the-box site through a service like Wix, Squarespace, or Wordpress. You can design your own website, or pay someone to custom-build one for you.

Make sure the look and feel of your website reinforces your visual aesthetic and personal brand, and tells the same story as your other application materials. For example, if you are applying for a Scenic Design apprenticeship but your website is solely focused on acting, with no mention of Scenic Design, a hiring manager is likely to disqualify you as you appear less genuinely interested than someone whose website has a Scenic Design section (yes, this really happens!). If you are a multihyphenate or are seeking jobs in different areas, think about how to organize your website to reflect this.

Your website can be a hub for connecting all your different multimedia and social media. It can aggregate your YouTube or Vimeo videos, blog, photo-sharing profiles, online stores, and professional social media accounts. You can also add the link to your website to your email signature, putting all of your multimedia, social media, and portfolio formats a click away in your correspondence.

All websites need:

- ◆ Contact information. If you don't want your email address to be visible, all website tools have the ability to create a webform. Make sure your webform connects to a working email address you check regularly.
- ◆ Information about your work. You can add a "resume" tab with your most up-to-date resume, add a bio, or do both. Remember that if you're a multihyphenate – like a director who is also a costume designer-- you need separate sections for each of your practice areas.
- ◆ Images and/or video. This can be as simple as one strong splash image on the main landing page, a photo gallery, or embedded video.

And that's it. Beyond that, you can choose to get as fancy and content-heavy as you'd like. Just keep it simple enough for anyone to easily find the information they're looking for. And remember: whatever you build, you need to maintain!

Thinking about a "blog" or "news" tab? Ask yourself if you are already a regular blogger, and if not, if it's a commitment you want to make. What about a "current projects" highlight on the home page? Just need to make sure it's always actually current and make a plan for moments when you're not working on anything. Want to add a "collaborations" tab but you're not sure what to put there so you just put "under construction"? Keep it hidden in draft mode until it's fully populated and ready to go.

When you're deciding on a website format and design, remember: **simple and up-to-date is far better than fancy and outdated**. Your website should be as easy to update as possible, and you need to commit to maintaining and regularly updating any section you create.

Social Media

Some creative individuals leverage social media presence to build their personal brand and share information in real time. It can be a faster and easier way to build an online presence than maintaining a website. You can choose to keep separate accounts for your personal life and your professional work, or find a balance with a single account. However, some people choose not to have a social media presence, often because of privacy concerns.

Creative professionals are often drawn to social media sites that primarily rely on visual content, like photos or videos. These can allow you to share more about your process, such as a series of short videos documenting the creation of a garment, or a hyper-lapse of a post-show strike. Tagging collaborators or the place where you're working can also help to expand your own network. Just be sure you always get permission to share any visuals from a project you're working on!

Some social networks, such as LinkedIn, are focused on professional networking and can be a helpful way to make new contacts. Know that all social media is likely to come up when someone searches for your name and use this to your advantage to continue building a strong brand.

It's a good idea to Google yourself regularly to get a sense of what prospective collaborators and employers see. As much as we would like to separate our personal and professional selves online, sometimes it's impossible – and you don't want a snarky comment or joke to cost you a major opportunity. Be thoughtful and professional in your online life, just as you are in a rehearsal room!

Submitting Your Materials

When you're ready to submit your materials for a job or opportunity, start by reviewing any submission instructions in the job description. There may be guidelines for how to name your files, what format to use, and even the correct email subject line.

If there aren't specific instructions, here are some best practices to follow.

- ◆ PDF your materials. This ensures that the person you're sending the materials to see the document exactly how you want them to

see it and that they can open it successfully. Note that other formats, such as Word files, may appear different depending on the recipient's computer and even what fonts they have installed. If you are a Mac user, remember that not all programs – including pages – are accessible on a standard PC. PDF is the safest way to submit your materials.
- Use clear and consistent file names that include your name. You can choose whether to also include the job title as well. "JSimpsonResume," "JuanSimpsonResume," or "JuanSimpson_LightingDesignResume" are all examples of acceptable file names.
- Do not link out to a cloud-based document, such as a document hosted on Google Drive, instead of providing an attachment, unless specifically requested to do so. This can require the employer to sign into a personal Google account and is an extra step. Don't make it harder on them!
- Stay professional in the email you send. Don't forget to include a subject line and write a message in the body of the email; it can be brief or you can choose to copy and paste your cover letter into the email as well as attaching it.

Triple-check that all your materials are the correct ones, named accurately, and successfully attached before hitting "send."

If you don't hear back for two weeks or so, it is appropriate to follow up to request an update on the status of your application.

And while you wait: stay positive. You never know what the process is on the other side of that application, and when you might get a phone call or email inviting you into the next phase of the job search: the interview!

Figure 5.2 Resume Worksheet.

Source: Created by Jessica Champagne Hansen using resources from Freepik.com and Macrovector.

Resume Worksheet

Description: Chapter 5 has great tips and suggestions for the layout and formatting of your resume, but what do you put in it? Use this worksheet to develop the content of your resume. When you finish, use this content to create your formatted and stylized resume. Note: Depending on your career and experience, you may not use all sections below.

Your Identification
Use your professional accounts for your resume.

Name	Phone	Email	Website

Production & Gig Work
List ALL experience in reverse chronological order. Use this "holding tank" for all experiences when you customize your resume.

Job Title	Production Name Special Event	Date	Production Co. Producer	Director	Venue

Part-time/Full-time Jobs
List ALL experience in reverse chronological order. Use this "holding tank" for all experiences when you customize your resume.

Job Title	Company	Description

Class Projects
If you are new to your field, list projects from classes/training that show your experience.

Project Name	Description	Details (date, location, production, etc.)

Figure 5.3 Resume Worksheet: Continued.

Source: Created by Jessica Champagne Hansen using resources from Freepik.com and Macrovector.

Resume Worksheet Continued

Education & Training
Fill in your education experience. Include your higher education, degrees, certificates, and specialty training.

College/University	City/State	Degree/Certificates

License Title	Training Location	Year

Specialty Training	Training Location	Year

Related Skills
Include all relevant and related skills. Include languages, hard skills, and software applications.

Awards & Accolades
List your awards, professional affiliations, and publications.

Personal Interests
This section is optional.

Professional References

Name	Job Title	Phone	Email

Career Marketing Materials ◆ 101

Figure 5.4 Portfolio Worksheet: Part I.

Source: Created by Jessica Champagne Hansen using resources from Freepik.com and Macrovector.

Portfolio Worksheet
Part I: Content

Description: Ready to create your professional portfolio? Part I of this worksheet will guide you through selecting five projects to showcase and deciding on important portfolio details. Then, we will inventory the content you have to include. After this worksheet, continue on to Part II: Layout.

Education & Training

Circle the answer(s) to the prompts below. You may circle more than one.

Portfolio Purpose:	Portfolio Type:	Portfolio Orientation:
School Interview Promotion	Website Print Digital	Portrait Landscape

Step 1: Evaluate

List your best 5 projects. They should show your skills, style, and process. Include all the project details.

A
B
C
D
E

Step 2: Ranking

Take those 5 projects from above and rank them in order from 1 to 5. 1 is your best work ever and 5 is great, but may not be seen due to time limits.

# 1	# 2	# 3	# 4	# 5

Step 3: Inventory

Take inventory of all the presentable visuals that you have from each project. Your inventory could include: Concept collages, concept text, research, sketches, renderings, paperwork, process photos, finished photos, material samples, and anything that supports your work.

1

2

3

4

5

Figure 5.5 Portfolio Worksheet: Part II.

Source: Created by Jessica Champagne Hansen using resources from Freepik.com and Macrovector.

Portfolio Worksheet
Part II: Layout

Description: This worksheet focuses on the layout of your portfolio. Use this sheet like a storyboard. Since you have 5 projects, make 5 copies of this page before you start, one for each project. In each box below, draw where you'd like your visuals, text, and titles. As you develop each page, remember the tips and suggestions in Chapter 5. Check out the sample box below!

Sample Page: Project Intro Page 1

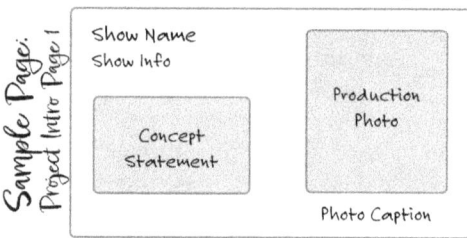

Show Name
Show Info

Concept Statement

Production Photo

Photo Caption

Project Intro: Page #1	Project Process: Page #2
Project Final Product: Page #3	Project Final Product: Page #4

Follow Up: The great thing about portfolios is that the process becomes easier the more you update and edit. Storyboarding can be used for a print portfolio, digital portfolio, and even your website. This is where it all comes together!

6

Interviews

Interview Overview

When you're called in for an interview for a job or gig you really want, your reaction might be joy, followed by fear. It's normal to feel nervous before (and during!) an interview. The more prepared you feel, the more you'll be able to conquer any nerves and approach an interview with confidence.

You should remember that you hold power in an interview. Creative consultant and live experience designer Andy Crocker has a healthy philosophy that she says applies to both interviews and casting processes for performers. Andy shares,

> Whether you are going into an audition or an interview, I think it is important to remember that the folks on the other side of the table are in a pickle. They are looking for someone to do a job. And, as luck would have it, you can do that job! You are there to offer a possible solution to their problem.

Remembering that you're there to help them can shift your attitude toward interviews from fear to confidence.

Even if you prepare thoroughly and do your best, the ultimate decision is out of your control. Sometimes, it's not a good fit, for any number of reasons. As Andy says,

DOI: 10.4324/9781003052227-9

Sure, there might be other solutions. They might choose someone else for one of a billion fair and unfair reasons, but in the end, you are just there to say, "Hi! I hear you are looking for someone! I'm a someone! Let's see if I can help you!"

You give them the gift of an interview with you and then leave the decision in their hands.

This chapter will provide strategies for interview preparation, including what to research, types of questions that might be asked, and how to negotiate a rate or salary. Note that we talked about informational interviews in the networking section; this chapter focuses on interviews for a specific job or opportunity, not the "get to know you" format of an informational interview.

We should mention that in our field, sometimes you'll be offered a job without an interview. Creative individuals, especially designers and technicians, can get jobs through their union, through their network, or in other nontraditional ways. This is particularly true for gig or project work. The number of jobs you score without a formal interview will likely increase as you move through your career.

However, at some point in the near future, you will find yourself preparing for an interview. Any position paid via salary or biweekly paycheck will likely require an interview process, as will jobs at a college or other educational institution. If you're planning on getting a "day job" or side job, note that the tips provided below can be used outside of the creative industries as well.

Even if an opportunity sounds like your dream job on paper, you need to use the interview to determine whether the projects, work culture, compensation, and expectations align with what you need. The activities in this chapter will help you identify what's important to you in a job setting, and how to address those needs and values during the interview process.

Types of Interview

Every interview process is unique. Sometimes, you will know exactly what you're walking into in advance; other times, you will need to be flexible and shift your strategy accordingly. For example, you might be provided with the names of interviewers, their positions at the organization, and the questions you'll be asked; or you may only receive a date and time to arrive. Visualizing different interview formats can help you feel more prepared, whether you walk into a room with one interviewer or ten!

The types of interviews listed below may be used individually or can be combined into a multistep process. An example would be an initial phone interview with one person, followed by a panel interview with a full team, and a final in-person, one-on-one interview with the executive director.

One-way video or audio interviews: These are primarily used as a first step in the interview process at larger companies. An applicant hears or sees an interview question on their computer screen and then has a set amount of time to respond while they are recorded. Usually, you cannot re-do your responses. This can be a particularly stressful format! Try to breathe, answer honestly, and smile.

Phone interviews: This is the most common format for initial interviews. It can be great for those who find it easier to express themselves without making eye contact. However, not being able to read the hiring manager's body language and facial expressions can make it harder to understand subtleties in tone, humor, and emotion. It may help to have a notebook in front of you during your interview where you write notes on the questions you're being asked to help keep you focused. Before you begin, find a quiet space with little to no ambient noise.

Group interviews: Sometimes employers will conduct interviews with many applicants at once. They can involve group discussions or even a shared task that applicants are asked to complete in teams. Group interviews evaluate applicants' interpersonal skills, such as the way they collaborate, listen, and problem-solve in a group setting. The best advice for this type of interview: try to focus on connecting with the other people in the room and bring your best attitude into the space.

One-on-one, in person, or via videoconference: An interview with one individual provides a great opportunity to make a deep connection. A great one-on-one interview feels like a conversation with both people getting to know one another and engaging in dialogue. Note that this goes for interviews conducted using video conference platforms, such as Skype or Zoom, which are becoming increasingly common. If you are doing a video interview, find a space where you won't be disturbed, and set up a neutral background; a sheet will work in a pinch.

Panel interviews: A panel interview gives you the opportunity to talk to several people from a department, project, or team at the same time.

You can learn a lot by observing team dynamics and can also get multiple perspectives on what interests you about a job or opportunity. Panel interviews can be difficult if you feel that one member of the panel is less engaged or involved than others; do make an effort to draw them out, but try not to let it distract you too much!

Whatever the format, it takes a lot of preparation to ace an interview. Let's talk about how to walk in ready to tell your story.

Preparing for Interviews

Once you know you have an interview scheduled, take a moment to celebrate and remember that there's a reason they selected you. You are qualified, ready, and would be a great asset to their team. The interview is not about proving anything: it's a conversation that allows you to share more about your skillset and ask questions.

However, nailing an interview requires research and careful preparation. We asked Merrianne Nedreberg, a Prop Director and artisan who has participated in many interview processes for designers and technicians, how she can tell whether an interview participant has done their homework. She says,

> You can tell who is prepared and who is not. The flow of answers is much more natural and allows for the interview to be more comfortable for both parties. Interviews become uncomfortable when the interviewer has to pull answers out of a candidate, and can feel like a waste of everyone's time.

Go into an interview armed with questions and eager to share your story.

Even if you spent time researching the company or organization when you submitted your application, go back, refresh your memory, and dive deeper. Look at the way they talk about themselves and their work on their website and social media. If it's a creative business, look at the art they make and think about why you're drawn to it. Merrianne notes,

> It is okay if you don't know much beyond what a company presents on its website, but you should be able to say why you want to work there. It is okay to say 'I don't know a lot about your company

from personal experience, but I did some research before I came and here is what I learned.' This opens the window for you to ask more questions and learn whether it is a good fit for you.

If you know the name of the person who will be interviewing you, research them too. If you haven't been provided with a name, you might be able to find a directory or staff listing online and make some guesses depending on where you'd be working. See if the people who might be interviewing you have presented at conferences, contributed to blogs, or have LinkedIn pages. Think about what priorities they might have and what you have in common. If this feels odd, remember they're researching you in the same way!

Speaking of which, this is a good moment to double-check your own online footprint. What comes up when you search for your name? Is your website as up-to-date as possible? Did your cousin just tag you in a photo you'd prefer a prospective employer didn't see?

Next, go back to the job description and re-read your cover letter and resume. Reflect on why you are the best one for the job. Think about how the combination of your background, skills, and experience align with what the job requires.

You can also consider your gaps, or the areas where you aren't as strong. These perceived weaknesses can cause anxiety when you're preparing for an interview. Instead of thinking about how to hide any areas where you don't check every box in the job description, practice what you'll say if directly asked about them. Where do you see equivalent experience in your background? How do you plan on enhancing your qualifications in these areas? If you don't have preferred computer knowledge, perhaps you can research training options and be prepared to say you'd take a class prior to starting the job. If you don't have a specific skill, such as teaching experience, think about how your past jobs have prepared you in nontraditional ways.

The more you role-play, the more comfortable you'll feel going into the real interview. Ask a friend to be the interviewer and give them the list of questions that stress you out the most. Practicing in a low-stakes environment gives you the opportunity to problem-solve and release anxiety before you get into the interview room.

If possible, you can also reach out to someone who has worked with the company, organization, and/or interviewer and ask them to chat with you. This is a great opportunity to get insider perspective. Note that everyone's personality and experiences are different, so their experience might not be your eventual experience – but it's helpful to get a window into the culture and structure of the place where you're interviewing.

It's Interview Time!

You've got this. On the day of the interview, make sure to eat, review any notes, and print out a hard copy of your resume and any other documents that have been requested if it's an in-person interview.

If you have a portfolio, bring it along, either in hard copy or on a tablet. It gives you an opportunity to talk about your work. Merrianne says, "I LOVE seeing your work and hearing you talk about it; it helps me see your skill and passion and helps me to imagine how you can fit in the job."

While few creative workplaces require a strict dress code, dressing "business casual" is a good strategy if you aren't sure how formal a workplace might be. If you're not sure what to wear, choose a comfortable outfit that is a more formal version of what you normally wear. Artists often express themselves with clothing and you want to feel like yourself in your clothes.

If you're feeling nervous, find a centering practice to bring yourself back to the present moment. This can be yoga, meditation, stretching, listening to a favorite song, or just taking a deep breath. Plan on arriving at the interview location early enough to do this practice.

In fact, just plan on arriving early. Don't let traffic cost you the interview. Remember that the interview starts before the interviewer begins asking questions: how you arrive (and whether you're on time!), how you greet them, and even your body language all start telling your story much earlier.

Above all, smile, make eye contact, and be yourself. Merrianne notes that an interview goes best

> When you are being your authentic self. Don't hold back your personality, don't wear something you wouldn't normally or that makes you uncomfortable, and share appropriate personal experiences. Part of an interview is seeing whether you fit in with the dynamic of that working environment, and if you hide your authentic self then you aren't allowing either yourself or the interviewer to really see if you are a good fit.

Common Interview Questions and Prompts

Once the interview begins, you'll quickly get a sense of the interviewer's style. Some interviews feel like casual conversations. Some are much more formal and may feel like the interviewer is following a strict set of guidelines.

If an interviewer asks a question that could be answered with "yes" or "no," think about how to expand on your answer.

The following questions and prompts are all frequently used in interviews. Some are specific to interviews at a creative workplace, such as a studio or theater, while others are much more general. They're presented in no particular order. Think about how you'd respond to each one.

- Tell me about yourself.
- What makes you a good employee? What do you bring to a workplace?
- What's your work style?
- Why did you leave your last job?
- What's your approach to your art? What's your creative process?
- We highly value anti-racism and equity, diversity and inclusion in this workplace. Can you talk about your beliefs and practices in this area?
- Tell me about a time you failed, and how you moved forward from that failure.
- Do you prefer working independently or in a team setting? Why?
- Tell me about a conflict you've had with another person, and how it was resolved (or wasn't!)?
- How do your skills and background align with this job/opportunity?
- Tell me about ____ on your resume. How was it working with ____?
- I went to the same college/training program/high school. Did you work with ____? What did you think of them?
- What's your general approach to conflict resolution?
- Why do you want to work here/with us?
- What draws you to the art we do? Have you seen/experienced it, and if so, what did you think?

- What's your favorite play or movie, and why? What about it resonates with you?
- What do you think makes a good leader? Do you see yourself as a leader?
- Describe your ideal working relationship with a boss. Do you prefer a boss to be more hands-on and collaborative, or do you prefer someone who gives you more space?
- How do you deal with pressure or stress in the workplace?
- What are your salary or payment requirements?
- What do you see yourself doing in five years? What are your career goals?
- What's something about your professional self you'd like to improve or change?

But what's the right answer? The right answer is your answer.

Say it with us: **the right answer is *your answer*.**

Trying to guess what the interviewer wants to hear to get the job hurts everyone. Be genuine and honest, and focus on answering the question instead of trying to make the interviewer happy.

While honesty is paramount, this doesn't mean you should bring your dirty laundry to an interview. This is particularly important related to past jobs or experiences. Remember that the creative industry is smaller than you think, and the professor you disliked or the boss you didn't get along with could be best friends with your interviewer. Think about reframing negative responses about specific people or organizations in a way that conveys what you want to say, without pointing fingers. Often, redirecting toward a positive experience is a way to move the conversation forward.

Example Question: I see you worked with Anya. How was that experience?

- What you want to say: She is totally disorganized and I spent six weeks trying to get her to respond to my emails. I'll never work with her again. At least the show was good.
- What you might really say: Oh yes, that was on the *Rock Candy* project. I loved that show. You know, that was my first time working in that theater. I'm not sure I'll get the opportunity to go back, but it's a great space. It actually led to my assistant design gig at the Guthrie the following year.

Example Question: Why did you leave your last job?

- What you want to say: It was a soul-sucking barren wasteland where dreams go to die.
- What you might really say: It felt like it was time for a new opportunity with more room to grow.

Example Question: What was your experience at College of the Mountains?

- What you want to say: Oh, the place where I racked up $15k of debt and learned absolutely no transferrable skills? I spent most of those two years chain-eating gummy bears and arguing with the financial aid office. So yeah. It sucked.
- What you might really say: I wasn't really involved with campus culture or the theater department. It was only after I transferred to Mountain University that I really found my passion for design.

Reframe, redirect, and keep things positive.

Also note that you should not be asked personal questions during an interview and should not feel pressured to share details about your life that are not relevant to the job. This includes information about your family or relationships, identity, friendships, or lifestyle.

Everyone's Least Favorite Question

You can probably guess the question people dread the most in an interview setting: "What's your biggest weakness?"

In our opinion, this is because it's a terrible and unnecessary question. It puts the applicant in a difficult position. It's very tempting to fall into the "what do they want to hear?" trap here, or try to invent a weakness that's actually a sneaky strength.

The best advice we have for this terrible question is to reframe it mentally as: "Where do you want to grow or learn, and how are you working toward that?" For example, if you feel like you'd love more leadership experience, perhaps you're committed to getting out of your comfort zone and stepping up to lead teams or speak in group settings. If you're working on your writing ability, perhaps you're thinking about taking a creative writing course, or are just focusing on slowing down and doing a spelling and grammar check every time you send an email.

This gives you an answer that's not only honest but also shows the interviewer that you approach your work from a learning mentality. And that, friends, is a strength.

Things You Should Ask and Dealbreakers

Many hiring managers believe that people being interviewed should ask good questions, instead of just answering them. Not having any questions can actually prevent you from being hired, as the person conducting the interview can interpret it as a lack of interest or inadequate research done into the job or opportunity.

It is also a critical part of the interview for you as a job-seeker. This is your opportunity to hear more about workplace culture and to lay the groundwork for self-advocacy. Think about what would make you excited to come to work every day and craft questions that will help you understand whether this job is the right one for you.

Sample questions about workplace culture:

- What do you love about working here/working on this project/working with this team?
- What's the work environment like, and what are the values of this workplace?
- What is this company's commitment to anti-racism/inclusion/equity/diversity?
- Do you feel like this company promotes health and wellness? If so, how?
- What is the orientation process like, and how are people welcomed into company culture?
- Do you feel like this company promotes learning and professional development for staff? If so, can you talk about what those opportunities look like?

You may also have questions specific to your needs and life. Before you get into an interview, reflect on whether there are any "dealbreakers" that should be addressed before a hiring process moves forward. A dealbreaker is something that would unequivocally prevent you from taking a position. Examples could be requirements around caregiving, other jobs or career commitments, unwillingness to travel extensively, or anything that might make you feel unsafe or unwelcome in a work environment. Do not try to discount your own needs during the interview process and hope to bring them up later, after you're offered the position.

You can choose whether to share why you're asking or to keep things general. This is a personal decision and can be complicated by your level of privilege, your career level, and many other factors. In the examples below, the italicized sentences could be omitted if the applicant did not want to name their personal relationship to each question.

Example Dealbreaker: You are seeking a flexible day job that allows you to continue pursuing your dream career in theater. You know without that flexibility, it's not the right day job for you.

Question to ask: "I understand this job provides flexibility in scheduling and few to no evening and weekend hours, based on the description. *This is important to me as I am a costume designer, and spend my evenings and weekends at the theater.* Can you speak to what flexibility in scheduling looks like?"

Example Dealbreaker: You are a caretaker to an elderly relative and need to be available for emergencies and leave promptly at 5 pm each evening.

Question to ask: "The job description says that this position is 9-5, and is a family-friendly workplace. *I have personal caretaking responsibilities that require me to keep my cell phone on, and sometimes step out to take calls. Occasionally I might need to leave early in an emergency situation.* Can you provide examples of how this workplace is family-friendly, and whether there is any variance in those regular hours?"

Example Dealbreaker: You are gender nonbinary and have experienced harm and aggressions in previous workplaces due to your identity. You need your next workplace to be different.

Question to ask: "Can you talk about the company's commitment to cultivating inclusive spaces? *As a nonbinary individual, this is important to me as it directly impacts my experience in the workplace.* I'm particularly curious about whether staff has mandatory training on gender inclusivity, and any recent changes the company has made to promote inclusion."

Pay close attention to those answers. If the interviewer seems reluctant to answer your questions, or if they seem irritated, cagey, or dismissive, you need to consider declining the opportunity or ending the interview.

See the "Reasons to Walk Away" section and the "What's Important to You?" worksheet at the end of this chapter to get more ideas about the kind of place you want to work and any dealbreakers you might need to address.

Let's Talk Money and Other Negotiations

It is perfectly appropriate for you to ask questions about compensation during an interview. This is particularly true if you aren't clear on a job's pay rate or range, or if you have questions about benefits. Even though we might be passionate about what we do, money is a necessity, and talking about it does not make you less of an artist. Don't apologize for asking about money. If they can't or won't answer questions about finances in early interviews, keep it in mind if you receive an offer and make sure you get full clarity before saying yes.

Before you get into the interview, you need to prepare to talk about compensation and understand exactly what you're seeking. If the job description didn't include exact pay or if you were approached directly and didn't see a description, it's critical for you to come with a number in mind that reflects your career level and many other factors, such as the cost of living in your area. There are various rate calculators online, as well as industry-specific charts that can give you an idea of what you make based on title, city, size of the organization or company, and various other factors.

There's a whole section on financial literacy coming up in Chapter 8, including contract negotiation and independent contractor best practices. If you're about to go into a negotiation, we suggest you flip to that section.

Other factors to ask about are whether benefits are included (e.g., health insurance, vision and dental, access to retirement plans like a 401K) and when they kick in, what the time off or vacation policy is, whether the job is flexible or not, and whether it will lead to more opportunities down the road. You may also consider whether the job will pay you as an independent contractor – meaning the amount you're being offered will be fully taxable – or if you are going on payroll and will have taxes taken out gradually. There's more on that in Chapter 8, too!

Artists may also consider whether the project is creatively exciting and sometimes choose to take a lower-paying opportunity because it feeds their artistic selves. That's a personal decision that can feel right for some.

Take care, though, that you're not being taken advantage of. Professionals need to be paid for their work and artists are not an exception.

When you're inquiring about compensation, benefits, or other aspects of the job, ask your questions clearly and don't feel like you need to explain why you're asking. Simply state your question and wait for their answer. If they reply by asking what you'd like to make or what your rate is, answer simply and clearly. Don't apologize. Don't over-explain. And above all, don't negotiate against yourself by adding phrases like "but I can be flexible" or "totally understand if that's not possible." Wait for them to respond.

If you do get an offer lower than what you want, you can counter-offer. Again, don't apologize, but be prepared to justify why you believe you need and deserve a higher amount. This can be related to your experience, standard wages or rates in your field, cost of living or transportation, or that you're already making more at another job. After you make the request, stop and wait for them to reply.

If the answer is yes, hooray! You advocated for yourself and stood up for what you're worth.

If the answer is no, pay attention to the reasoning. Sometimes wages or rates are standardized within an organization, so there are equity reasons why they can't bring in a new person at a higher rate than someone who's been in the position for a year or more. Sometimes the hiring manager may say they only have the given amount for the position but would be able to advocate for a raise in six months or a year. They should not be defensive or dismissive; payment negotiation is a healthy and normal part of the job process.

Then, it's up to you to decide whether you do want to take the job or if you prefer to walk away. Knowing the lowest acceptable rate before you walk into the interview can help you be prepared if you do need to decline and end the interview.

Negotiation is a key skill for those in the creative industry. Learning to stand up for yourself and your worth can help you build a stronger career, faster.

Following Up

On the same day as your interview, send a thank-you note. This can be via email or a physical note you drop in the mailbox. The note should be brief but can reference one or two points of connection from the interview or conversations you particularly enjoyed. Keep it professional but reiterate your interest in the opportunity.

And then, the waiting begins. If the interviewer didn't give you a timeline for when you might hear back from them, you might feel like you're in limbo. If you don't hear anything for two weeks, it's appropriate to send a follow-up email or call to check in.

However, after the interview, there is little to do but wait. You have no idea what's happening internally, and trying to guess what the employer is thinking is impossible. Remember Andy Crocker's philosophy: you offered to help them solve their problem. Now the decision is up to them.

Reference Checks

A prospective employer checking your references is a great sign. Usually, this indicates you are among the top candidates for an opportunity. It is most common for reference checks to happen either immediately before or immediately after a final interview.

As soon as you have your first interview, reach out to your references if they're listed on your resume and give them a heads-up that they might be contacted. If you've chosen to have your references available upon request, you can wait until you provide that information to alert your cheerleaders that they're likely to be contacted.

Send your references your most current resume, the job description, and anything you would love for them to talk about. For example, if the job requires strong mentorship skills, you can ask your former boss to bring up how you worked with interns and apprentices. These folks are there to support you, and they will be eager to get any information that will help them provide an excellent reference.

Hearing a No

"I'm sorry, we are going with another applicant." Ouch. That response can sting.

You will hear a lot of "no" in your career. All of us do, particularly in the competitive creative fields. It can be helpful to try to reframe a "no" as "not right now, not this opportunity, not this company." It's not a no, forever.

If it's possible to ask for feedback on your interview and materials, do it. It can help you get additional perspective on why you weren't selected. Sometimes it's something easily fixable, like forgetting to mention you have carpentry experience or being too casual or too formal in your interview.

Whether or not you receive feedback, there may be other factors beyond your control that impacted their decision-making. Sometimes there are internal candidates poised for promotion. Sometimes another applicant brings an unusual or different skillset. And sometimes, there's just someone else who's more qualified or more enthusiastic about the job than you—and that's okay. You will find your own best fit.

Finally, you never know when an interview will pay off further down the road. It's more common than you might think for an interviewer to reach out to you months or even years later with another opportunity. This is why it's important to thank them and express continued interest in working with them!

Reasons to Walk Away

Sometimes, it's going to be you who says no to a job offer. Here are a few common reasons why you might need to decline an opportunity or position.

The pay is too low. If negotiation doesn't work and the salary or payment won't work for you, you need to respectfully decline. Beware the promise of a pay increase in the future – unless you get it in writing.

The job is different than what you wanted or expected. Sometimes the interview provides additional information about an opportunity that makes you second-guess whether it's the right fit. Occasionally, an employer may literally offer you a different – usually lower-paying – job than what you initially applied for. Trust your instinct if you feel you've been a victim of a bait-and-switch, or if you just misunderstood what the job would be.

You realize you just … don't want it. Never go into an application process just for fun, or to "practice" your job search skills; it's disrespectful to the company or organization and can hurt your reputation. However, it is common for people to apply for a job with good intentions but realize along the way that they're actually happier in their current position or just don't feel passionate about the opportunity. It is okay to change your mind and withdraw.

You see other red flags. Has anything been … *off* during the interview process? Do the people, office culture, or circumstances make you feel uncomfortable? Do you feel like information about payment, benefits, or other aspects of the job are being withheld from you or hidden? Do you feel you're being tokenized or taken advantage of? Trust your gut. If something feels off, it probably is.

If you need to decline a position, do it promptly and clearly. Don't leave them in suspense longer than you need to. Provide the declination in writing. You can decide whether to give your reasons or to just say you're no longer interested.

When to Say Yes

Let's say you get that dream phone call or email: Congratulations! We'd love to offer you the gig. Do your silent happy dance, pump your arms in the air, and then:

Don't say yes.

At least not immediately. Instead say, "**Thank you so much**! I'm extremely interested in this opportunity. How much time do I have to get back to you with an answer?"

Jumping into a "yes" is so tempting, especially if it's a dream job. Before you commit, though, you need to take a moment to be sure you have the information you need and have done your due diligence with current employers and key people in your life.

Before you accept, make sure you address all of the factors below. There may be others you need to add.

- ◆ Do you have all of the information about the job's requirements, start date, benefits, payment, any accommodations you want or need, and any "dealbreaker" items? If not, what do you need to ask for?
- ◆ Are there any non-negotiable dates you need to check with the new employer before committing to the job, such as your graduation or wedding?
- ◆ If you have a current employer, do you want to give them the opportunity to counter-offer before you accept the new position? **Don't skip this step if the issue with your current position is too little money or lack of promotion.** Unfortunately, sometimes it

takes an external offer for a company to recognize your worth and promote you.
- ◆ If you've applied to other jobs, do you want to check-in on those application processes first? This is important if the job offer you get isn't your first choice.
- ◆ Are there key people you need to talk to before you accept the position? An example would be a spouse who'd need to relocate with you if you took a new job.

After you've run through that list and feel confident that the job is right for you, then it's time to say yes. Do so clearly and unequivocally, and request all information about compensation, start dates, and benefits in writing.

Visualizing that moment of accomplishment can help you get through that 1:30 am personal website redesign or awkward phone interview. It's all worth it when you get to jump into a creative community and do what you love.

In the next section, we'll talk about how you can build on that community and deepen your relationships with other creative professionals.

Figure 6.1 What's Important to You? Interview Worksheet.

Source: Created by Camille Schenkkan and Jessica Champagne Hansen using resources from Freepik.com and Macrovector.

What's Important to You?
Interview Worksheet

Description

Use this worksheet to prepare for any interview process. Before you start, review the sections "Things You Should Ask" and "Let's Talk Money" in Chapter 6.

I want to work in an environment where I feel _____

When it comes to duties and tasks at work, I prefer _____

I struggle with or don't like work environments where _____

I believe my greatest professional strengths are _____

My ultimate career goal is _____

The best position to help me achieve that career goal would be, provide, or involve _____

My ideal rate or pay range is _____

My hourly rate or pay range must be at least _____
Under that amount, I will walk away and decline the position.

The benefits that I need are _____

My non-negotiable dealbreaker items are _____

In an interview, I will ask about those dealbreaker items using the following questions: _____

Follow Up

Re-visit this sheet before each interview process and update as needed.

Part III
Curating a Creative Community as You Sustain Your Career

7

Unions, Organizations, Groups, and Publications

Your Creative Community

A career is more fulfilling when you are surrounded by supportive professional colleagues that you cultivate along your way. This creative community is more than your personal network: it includes groups and organizations that help to champion and support you and your work. Unions, organizations, virtual and in-person groups, trade publications, and conferences all inspire you to learn more, aim higher, and push your creative boundaries.

Each of these creative communities has distinct benefits – personal, professional, or economic. Some of these groups are open to all, while others are by application only. Some require entrance fees and annual dues; others are free. Being an active part of these communities may happen by necessity or circumstance, or you may actively set the goal to become a member.

In this chapter, we'll focus on the unions and support organizations in the industry, outlining the benefits, how to join, and professional perspectives. We'll also touch on other ways to build community, including online groups and special publications.

DOI: 10.4324/9781003052227-11

Overview of Unions

A union is an organized group of workers from the same industry focused on representing the interests of the members. Unions are a community. Being a union member means that you have the support of fellow members and the union itself, and can be a way to create lasting connections. You may decide that you'd like to take your involvement in the union community further, and you can run for an elected leadership position. This is a great way to advocate for your craft and colleagues on a larger scale, making change for the whole community.

What Do Unions Do?

There are numerous benefits to union membership, including collective bargaining, health insurance and retirement, and employment support. But how do they work and what do they do for their members? We will break down the main professional and personal benefits of becoming a union member.

Collective Bargaining

Collective bargaining refers to a group of employees and/or union members negotiating with the employers to establish pay scale, benefits, processes (such as grievance procedures in case you experience harm), guidelines for safety and health at work, and more. This means that if you are a union member or are otherwise a part of a collective bargaining agreement, your contracts with your employer are predetermined at a certain minimum rate with specific details. We will be talking more about contracts and how they vary based on union status and industry in Chapter 8. You are also protected by specific protocols and processes intended to keep you safe in the workplace.

Each local union negotiates contracts and supports its members in different ways, which means that union agreements vary based on location.

In an industry where pay can fluctuate dramatically, it is a relief to know that as a union member, you will earn a negotiated rate. This can take a lot of the stress out of freelancing but does not mean that you do not need to be financially literate and advocate for pay equity. It is up to all of us to stand up for ourselves, our colleagues, and our field.

Health Insurance and Retirement

As a union member, you will be able to receive health insurance and retirement benefits. Be sure to research the plans specific to your local union, as they vary. These benefits are often offered with guidelines that you need a certain number of union work hours each year to qualify. We strongly recommend thinking about these benefits – including retirement – sooner, rather than later. A month turns into a year, and then a decade, with no savings or safety net. Plan proactively, instead of reactively.

Employment Support

A common misconception about being a union member is that you are automatically "sent out" for work and will quickly have full-time employment without having to engage in self-promotion or networking. This is false; a union is not your agent (and even those who have an agent still need to take a role in their career growth!). Unions often have Availability Lists, which all union members looking for employment can join, and employers can view. However, you will still be spending time networking, applying, interviewing, and looking for your next opportunity. Another misconception is that union members are full-time employees at a company. This can be true, but the union is also full of freelance artists, making full-time employment out of numerous jobs.

As we have said in previous chapters, you will be learning new things your whole career. A union is a great way to stay up-to-date with education and professional development. Unions offer short-term courses, especially in safety, and send out publications with articles from members and industry partners on current best practices and trends.

> **A note about Agents: You may get to a point in your career with high-profile projects where you need an agent to assist and support you. An agent represents you both in finding work and in contract negotiations. This can relieve you of the stress and time required for those tasks but remember you will be paying the agent directly from each check that you receive for those projects. When you feel you are ready for representation, talk with colleagues for advice and input.**

How to Join a Union

Every union – and local union chapter – has different qualifications and procedures for becoming a member. These will be listed on their website and available at the union's offices.

Unions all require at least one of the following for prospective members:

- Previous skills and experience
- Entrance exam, portfolio review, and/or skills demonstration
- Application process and fee
- References

If you are accepted into the union, congratulations! Remember that you may need to pay initiation dues, in addition to the first installment of your annual dues. Ask about the pay schedule in advance so you're not surprised by that first invoice.

Can you be a member of more than one union? Yes, you can! This is called a dual-card membership. Just remember that there will be two different annual dues and sets of requirements. Although most readers of this book are pursuing fields captured within IATSE, some of you will be a part of another union. For example, if you are in a teaching position, you will probably become a member of the American Federation of Teachers (AFT) or a similar teachers' union.

Union Spotlight: The International Alliance of Theatrical Stage Employees (IATSE)

In the United States and Canada, almost all union jobs involving designers and technicians are covered by IATSE. IATSE has represented workers since 1893. It is the largest union in our field and, as stated on its website, the "members work in all forms of live theater, motion picture and television production, trade shows and exhibitions, television broadcasting, and concerts, as well as the equipment and construction shops that support all these areas of the entertainment industry." So, if you are a union stagehand for theater, a union costume designer in film, or a union lighting board operator traveling with a show, you will be part of IATSE.

Within IATSE, there are 375 local unions, related by location and type of work or craft. These are called "locals," and each has a number designation. For example, Local 800 in IATSE is the Art Directors Guild, representing Art Directors, Illustrators, and Matte Artists, Set Designers and Model Makers, and Scenic, Title and Graphic Artists in entertainment working in the US, Canada, and internationally.

Some unions are not just craft-specific, but also location-specific. For example, Local 33 Stagehands and Projectionists is in Los Angeles, and Local 1 represents New York City Stagehands. Membership can transfer but again may have different requirements, benefits, and processes.

Other Unions

Although IATSE is the largest union in entertainment for designers and technicians, there are many other unions involved in the creative industries. You might find yourself as a member of the Teamsters union if you are working on locations in film and television. If you branch out into other jobs, you may need to join other unions, such as the Director's Guild of America. Also, if you work internationally, you will find that different countries have their own industry unions.

Nonunion Life

You will almost all start your career as a nonunion worker, since most unions require a certain amount of previous work experience in order to apply for membership. There are many benefits to working as a nonunion freelancer, and many decide to remain that way for their whole careers, as there are many job opportunities in entertainment that do not require union membership.

Being a freelancer is like being an entrepreneur! You are in charge of everything, which could be exactly what you are looking to do. This is great if you have multiple areas of interest and a varied skillset. You will be managing your own schedule, work opportunities, health insurance, retirement, and so on. You have the freedom to create the best work environment for you. Of course, this requires a high level of organization, proactivity, and planning.

Benefits of Nonunion Life

Nonunion work often allows for freedom in your schedule, a chance to be an entrepreneur, travel, a variety of jobs, and more (although sometimes a full-time nonunion job does not allow for these). JM Montecalvo is a freelance nonunion Lighting Designer, who is also the President and CEO of his own company. He loves nonunion freelance life and shares,

> The first time that I worked as a lighting designer, it was both liberating and terrifying. I had the freedom to accept only the jobs that interested me. However, I was so hungry to work that I did everything lighting had to offer. I started by running cable and hanging lights, working my way up until someone let me run crews and design a project.

Staying nonunion let him continue to explore different roles and take jobs at any company.

JM went on to start his own lighting firm and says, "with control of my own company, I was able to attract all types of lighting projects and attractions, from Nighttime Studio Tour at Universal Studios Hollywood to Marvel Avenger Stations attractions in China, Singapore, and Russia." Throughout his career, he chose to remain nonunion:

> I had a few chances to join one, but by the time those opportunities came along, I was working consistently outside of the union space. I don't think there is anything wrong with joining a union. In fact, I think that unions offer more job security, but for me, I think the limitations may outweigh the benefits.

This freedom is an attractive part of freelancing, and nonunion work often allows for the most flexibility.

Challenges of Nonunion Life

A nonunion freelance artist is an entrepreneur. They need to manage finances, marketing, and the complexities of running a business, whether they operate independently or start their own company, like JM did. Nonunion freelancers also represent themselves in negotiations around contracts and pay. JM notes,

It's a high-wire act and without a union, you are your own safety net. There were a few times I wished I had a union to back me up but without it, I have learned to trust my instincts and stand my ground.

We mentioned in the section about Unions that you will still need to do most of the work to find your next jobs. Of course, the same is true if you are not represented by a union. JM enjoys the hustle but acknowledges its difficulty: "The hardest part is finding the work; you have to be very proactive all the time. Every new person you meet is a potential referral and every project is an interview for the next one." He adds that word of mouth and your performance are the greatest drivers for new business. JM says,

> Most of our big opportunities were the result of a direct referral from either past clients or other professionals and companies that we had previously collaborated with. A trusted relationship with a colleague or client can propel you further than thousands of dollars in marketing.

Union or not, the power of reputation is a major driver in the entertainment field.

Should I Join a Union?

The question of whether or not you should join a union is complex and needs to take into account your career level and goals, location, and whether you feel like you are being held back from work you would otherwise qualify for. A union can certainly support your career, but union membership shouldn't necessarily be something to work toward without considering these other factors.

The decision to join a union may be essentially made *for* you, when you accept a certain job. Some entire industries, like network television, require that you are a union member, except in the case of certain entry-level positions. Other industries, like theater, have many positions that do not require union membership, and some that do. Like JM, you may choose to work most or all of your career as your own employer or run your own company, and this option to join a union may present itself along the way.

This is one of those doors that will open when the timing is right. At the end of this chapter, there is a worksheet with questions to help you answer this question. In addition to completing the worksheet, we recommend visiting unions' websites and talking to some of their members about the benefits and challenges. Similarly, the best way to learn about working as a nonunion member is to talk to someone currently running their own company and/or freelancing.

> **Jess here! I have worked half of my career in a union, and half without. Since I was a student, I wanted to be union because I wanted that super cool stamp to put on my renderings! I really believed the stamp would prove that I was "official." Well, my career started picking up even without the stamp, and becoming a union member fell lower on my priority list because it wasn't the right time. After having two children, I felt like the theater community forgot that I was still a capable and available designer and not just a mom. I applied for and joined the union because I needed the support of a community of colleagues. Also, I really did want that stamp! Union membership is a personal decision and can happen in any phase of your career.**

No matter what you choose, all pathways require financial knowledge, time management, and other key skills (Chapter 8 will address all these topics). JM reminds us that

> No matter whether you choose union or nonunion, freelance or full-time work, only hard work will make you successful; there's just no easy way to success. My dad always told me to pay attention to everything because you never know when you might need to know something.

Just keep navigating and paying attention. The decision to join or not join a union will reveal itself along the way.

Benefits of Professional Organizations and Groups

Service organizations, trade groups, advocacy organizations, and lobbying coalitions all exist to support healthy, sustainable careers in our field. Organizations have different structures and are of varying sizes but share the same goal of making their members and the workplace better.

From theme parks to technical theater, there are organizations that help to support, connect, and educate members in different fields of entertainment and craft areas. For example, the Themed Entertainment Association (TEA) is an organization for designers, storytellers, producers, consultants, and more from the themed entertainment industry. The Educational Theatre Association (EdTA) supports theater educators, at all grade levels, nationally and internationally. If you have a niche, there is probably an organization made for you!

Many of these groups are membership organizations. Some organizational memberships are free, and others charge an annual fee. It is important to research their benefits before deciding if it is a good time in your career to pay for membership. This investment might be an excellent one if you're a student or young professional, helping you bridge your experiences from education to the industry. Many organizations have specific groups for young professionals and discounted pricing for membership.

When you're shopping for a professional organization to join, here are some of the membership benefits you might read about. Think about what you're looking for at this phase in your career.

Continuing Education

Like unions, professional organizations often offer affordable classes, workshops, and training to members. These courses can be broad, like portfolio techniques, or very specific, like special effects makeup application. Any additional training directly benefits you with marketable skills and a chance to network and create relationships with industry colleagues.

Job Boards and Directories

Many groups have job boards exclusively for members, which is beneficial in an industry where most jobs are spread through word of mouth and networking. These job boards post specific job opportunities that align with the skills and craft specialties of its members. When you join an organization, you often make a profile with information about your career experience. Many organizations have a membership directory of their members, to help connect you to job opportunities.

Commissions and Working Groups

These groups also offer commissions organized by craft which meet periodically to discuss the future of their field, connect members in similar jobs, and study together in summits and symposiums. These commissions within the organization are a great way to get involved more in your craft. Another benefit of an organization is the opportunity for grant and fellowship funding to support your professional projects as you push the boundaries of your field.

Networking, Conferences, Events, and Study Tours

Many organizations hold annual conferences with meetings, classes, expos, and more. While anyone can attend conferences and special events, organization members receive discounted tickets and early registration. Conferences and events are a great venue for networking, which we have discussed already in earlier chapters. Proposing to lead a conference session is another great way to enhance your visibility as a rising star in your career path!

Conferences can be local, national, or international. Prague Quadrennial of Performance and Design Space is an example of an international event, which is held every four years, celebrating performance, design, and theater. Similarly, World Stage Design is held every four years as a showcase for performance design from individual designers. The Southeastern Theatre Conference (SETC) is an example of a regional organization that has an annual conference and special events.

Some groups may offer additional events year-round, or even a members' "study tour," like a trip to Europe to study fabric fabrication. Sign me up! Once you are an organization member, you'll receive information about member-exclusive conferences, events, and study tours.

Advocacy and Lobbying

There is strength and power in numbers. Many service organizations engage in advocacy and even direct lobbying, helping to shape public policy and share important information to keep you safe, healthy, and employed. Joining an organization that engages in advocacy – or just getting on their email list and taking action when prompted – is a great way to make a difference, for yourself and others.

> **A note for Professors and Educators:** Educators balance our commitment to education and our students with our own contributions and involvement in the industry. Organizational membership is a great way to connect with both sides of your professional practice. Workshops, commissions, and conferences provide a way to stay involved with your industry and practice your craft.

Publications

Publications are a convenient and concise way to explore new ideas and emerging trends in your field and keep you connected to your creative community. Unions and organizations use publications to showcase individual work, highlight emerging technologies, and share new perspectives in our fields. Many publications are both digital and printed magazines, which are a convenient way to connect during our busy schedules. You can stash an industry publication in your carry-on and catch up on your reading while you fly to your next gig.

There is often a publication and a newsletter focused on keeping its members up-to-date and informed. USITT, for example, has a membership web-based newsletter called *Sightlines* as well as a quarterly magazine called *TD&T* (*Theater Design & Technology*) offered both online and in print. Another example of an organizational publication is *American Theatre* magazine, from Theatre Communications Group (TCG).

A great benefit of industry publications is having the opportunity to have your own work published. Publishing broadens your professional experience and allows you to share your expertise with your colleagues. If you are a professor in higher education, publishing is an important step in your career.

> **Note from Jessica:** Writing has been one of the greatest challenges of my career. I am so thankful to my mentors for encouraging me to try writing. Start by writing an article and see where it takes

> you! Look for opportunities in your union or in organizations for sharing your writing. Everyone has a story to tell, and your experiences will be helpful for so many fellow colleagues and readers.

Organization Spotlight: United States Institute for Theatre Technology (USITT)

If you are interested in a career in the creative design and technical fields, it is highly likely you will eventually be connected to USITT, one of the largest organizations in the entertainment industry. Founded in 1960, the organization connects designers, technicians, educators, students, vendors, publishers, and more. Their charter, according to their website, is to "promote dialogue, research, and learning among practitioners of theater design and technology." Some of what they provide is free, and they also offer multiple levels of memberships and fees.

Like any organization, there are many ways to get involved with USITT, and a variety of benefits. These include education and training, a job board, and discounts on professional tools such as books and products. The organization has numerous venues for showcasing your work, both online and at the annual conference and expo. Throughout the year, members receive notification about grants and fellowship applications as well as awards and organization recognitions.

The annual conference provides a great opportunity for education and networking in live entertainment, at any stage of your career. Focused on new technologies and connection opportunities, the conference features professional development workshops and a stage expo to connect theater artists with specialty vendors and companies. The conference also provides opportunities for young professionals and students to meet with industry mentors for portfolio reviews and interviews. Finally, the conference marks the announcement of numerous professional awards and recognitions, which help individuals to continue pushing limits and striving for growth in their career journey. Ashley Bellet, the Vice President for Commissions at USITT and Associate Editor for Education for their *Theatre Design & Technology* publication, encourages early-career individuals to get involved in USITT even outside of the annual conference:

> That conference or event is just one part of the larger organization – most are working 365 days to support you and the theater community in lots of ways. Take advantage of that, recognize that, and find a place where you can contribute.

Ashley notes that just like everything else in our field, there's a potential to overcommit yourself when working with a professional organization or group, and you need to set clear boundaries for your involvement. She says,

> This protects your time AND your reputation within the organization. This goes back to the concept of authenticity – you have to be clear about what you want and need, just as the organization should be clear about what they expect from you.

Balance and support are important factors if you choose to become more involved in the community of organizations, such as USITT.

Online Groups and Communities

Online groups and communities are a great arena for connecting with colleagues from all over the world. Social media platforms often have organized groups by region and craft, with the goal of connecting artists for advice, job opportunities, and sharing resources. Some groups are open to the public and others are private with a host that reviews your request to join.

Lighting Designer Emily Bornt manages a group called Wom+n In the Entertainment Industry on Facebook. She was inspired to start the group while touring.

> I was meeting other women in my industry who felt alone and outnumbered, so I created a Facebook group to bring them together and build a community. It was a very simple thing to do and has helped build some really great connections between the members. When I need to find someone to fill a role on a show, I can put up a post and know that it's a group of qualified readers who are responding, and I am able to look at their profiles and

> mutual friends and help figure out if they are a good fit to the type of project or general vibe of the client.

An online group is a creative way to take the job announcement traditionally spread by word of mouth and share it more immediately on social media and with a broader group.

Online presence is an important part of staying visible in your field, and these groups are a great way to connect without the commitment of a formal membership with an organization.

> It serves as an opportunity to offer support to those who post about any issues they may be having locally and is a place to share positivity and inspiration. For me, one of the most fulfilling parts is watching members become really involved and help others,

shares Emily.

How Do You Build Community?

Think about how you want to connect with your colleagues and industry, whether it's online, one-on-one, or at a large event like a conference. Continuing to learn from colleagues and strengthen your connections is a crucial element of a thriving creative career.

As a community, we are all stronger when we ensure that everyone has the skills and strategies to be successful in entertainment. Whether you are union or nonunion, you need solid strategies to move your career forward. These include building skills in money management, time management, and more! We will discuss these topics in Chapter 8 on surviving and thriving in your creative career.

Figure 7.1 Union or Nonunion?

Source: Created by Jessica Champagne Hansen using resources from Freepik.com and Macrovector.

Union or Non Union?

Description: What is best for you right now: working as a union member or nonunion member? Answer the following questions by circling your response from the options in each column.

	Union	Hybrid	Non Union
Right now, most of my work is...	Union	Hybrid	Non Union
I am comfortable arranging all of my benefits, like health insurance and retirement.	I'd like help	Yes and No	Yes
Currently, I can afford union fees and dues.	Yes	Sometimes	No
I can arrange and negotiate my contracts, payment, and rate scale.	I'd like help	Yes and No	Yes
The jobs that I aspire to require union membership.	Yes	Yes and No	No
I am looking for union support to network, receive education, and find jobs.	Yes	Yes and No	No
After researching local unions, I am now qualified to apply to the union.	Yes	Not yet	No
I have an entrepreneurial spirit and wish to manage all aspects of my career.	No	Sometimes	Yes
I aspire to or currently work in multiple industries and fields at the same time.	No	Varies	Yes

Follow Up: When you are finished, observe which column you circled the most for your answers. Did you circle mostly union? Time to look into the requirements for joining. Did you circle mostly nonunion? Maybe now is not the best time to join. Did you circle mostly hybrid? Looks like you are still in-between and you can revisit this worksheet in a year or so.

8

Creative Career Surviving and Thriving Skills

Not Just Surviving, but Thriving!

When we think about training for a creative career, we focus on craft and technique: the artistic and technical skills we use day-to-day as designers, technicians, or managers. However, there is a separate skillset crucial to building a sustainable career in this sometimes chaotic, always exciting field. Regardless of whether you're a life-long freelance artist or if you spend your career in a full-time job, the skills we discuss in this chapter will be key to your success – and, more importantly, to your happiness and well-being.

We'll start with financial empowerment: getting comfortable managing your money, creating and negotiating contracts, doing your taxes, and even saving for retirement. Next, we'll explore strategies for time and project management, including what to do between gigs, and how to say "no" to projects that aren't right for you.

Preparation is key to thriving as a creative artist in entertainment. You may have been drawn to these careers because you wanted to choose your projects and have a high degree of creative freedom. This autonomy comes with big responsibilities. You are often your own marketing manager, financial planner, social media strategist, and agent. This is a lot to juggle, but with some strategies and planning, you will thrive, instead of just survive.

DOI: 10.4324/9781003052227-12

Financial Literacy vs. Financial Empowerment

"Financial literacy" means that you can talk about, manage, and engage in thoughtful planning related to money. Financial literacy for creative careers includes personal budgeting, negotiating contracts, tracking work-related expenses, using financial resources and tools, and setting financial goals.

If these topics make you anxious or uncomfortable, you're not alone. There are serious and complex social, emotional, and cultural reasons why we find it hard to think and talk about our finances. We may hold trauma connected to money; those of us whose parents struggled with their financial health may find it difficult to separate our emotions from the experiences of our families.

This is why we like to use the phrase **financial empowerment** instead of financial literacy. Instead of purely *understanding* your finances, we want you to feel *empowered* to make healthy choices that best support your financial goals. You can be creative and also want a steady paycheck, and you can be a gig worker who isn't a "starving artist." You can also change your financial goals at any time as you advance in your career or move into different phases of your life.

Elena Muslar, a creative career coach and workforce development consultant specializing in arts, culture, and entertainment equitable practices, works with her clients to achieve personal **financial liberation**, or the freedom of knowing your financial situation is stable, healthy, and will provide you with the lifestyle you want to live. She says,

> I lean more toward prioritizing strategic planning conversations around financial liberation (what it SPECIFICALLY looks like, sounds like, feels like, and even acts like) in which financial literacy is a touchpoint so that those I work with can move past scarcity mind sets and toward tangible wealth-building action items.

Taking the time to think about what financial success looks like is crucial and can help you create a roadmap to get there.

It's a major, systemic issue that financial management – especially personal money management – is not included in most training programs for the creative industries, when it is an essential part of career success. Many people leave entertainment fields, especially the theater, because of a lack of financial literacy training compounded by the difficult, and sometimes predatory or toxic, financial realities of the field. As Elena says,

> Financial intimidation due to lack of access to information is the hurdle many have to jump over if they truly want to get to a point where they aren't just sliding by as creative hobbyists in disguise but instead are choosing to walk through previously unopened doors as creative professionals with their heads held high.

Those with additional challenges, including parenting or caretaking, significant debt or family pressure, may be even more likely to change careers because of a lack of access to financial training and resources.

If you aren't prepared to advocate for yourself or aren't aware of the value of your art and skill, you can also be taken advantage of. There is a long-standing history of entertainment professionals accepting low wages or even working for free in the hopes that a sacrifice in pay will lead to greater opportunities in the future. The story we have told ourselves is that we won't get the job if we ask for too much, that it will look selfish to ask for an equitable wage, or that there will always be someone else who *will* take the job for less pay. It's a vicious cycle tied to systemic inequity and lack of access for people from marginalized backgrounds. Elena agrees:

> One of the biggest pieces of advice I have found myself often repeating is that it is truly possible to hurdle over that demeaning 'starving artist' stereotype, which has usually been ingrained into creative psyches by societal/parental assumptions based on very little current awareness of just how robust the creative economy really is and actually leap toward becoming a 'thriving artist' if you can get clear on your financial plans, break those down into steps, then align them with your creative career goals – in that order.

Remember:

◆ It is normal and healthy to discuss, ask for, and value money. It doesn't make you less of an artist. Money is a necessity for all of

us, and very, very few of us have the luxury to "not care about money."
- Having a "day job" or taking on work outside of the creative industries also doesn't make you less of an artist. Rather, a portfolio career with multiple sources of income can help you build a sustainable life in the arts, particularly in your first few years out of school.
- Compensation shouldn't be a secret or a taboo topic when you are applying for or even being offered a job. Employers should provide compensation up-front, ideally in a job posting, and certainly in an initial interview. Asking about benefits, time off, and other financial aspects of a job or opportunity is normal and necessary.
- You should be paid for work you are asked to do. And your creativity, artistry, and passion alone do not pay your rent. While you can decide to take on volunteer work as passion projects, this should be on your terms and done freely. If you feel you're being taken advantage of, you have the power to step away.

Taking small, incremental steps, like downloading a budget-tracking app or doing 15 minutes of online research into savings strategies, can help you begin to address fear or anxiety around money. If you find yourself struggling to discuss or think about finances, you might consider talking to a financial therapist, a counseling professional who specializes in trauma and emotion connected to money.

Doing this work is worth it. Elena notes, "I have found that more often than not, the difference between creative dreamers and creative doers is based around how much confidence they have developed in the reliability of their cash flow, not necessarily their creative direction." Being confident in your finances can help you thrive as an artist.

Your Budget Is Your Blueprint

Having a budget for your personal life and professional career is just as important as the budget you create for your multi-million-dollar design project. The ideal difference between your income and expenses is a personal decision that can guide your career and lifestyle choices. In the simplest terms, you just need to make sure that you are making more than you are spending.

To go a little deeper, a budget is a reflection of your values. Understanding what's most important to you can help you design a budget that supports not only career success, but fulfillment and joy in all areas of your life. Getting familiar with how you're spending your money now can help you start to plan for how you want your finances to look 10, 20, or 50 years down the road. Even if you don't feel like you want or need a lot of money, you may enjoy travel, hobbies, or dream about starting a family or owning a home.

And if you DO want a lot of money, rock on. There are certainly areas of the creative industries that pay very well. Understanding how much you'd like to make and researching what jobs can provide that income level will help you make career decisions. Whether we like it or not, money must be a part of our decision-making process.

Whatever your financial goals, budget-tracking forms or spreadsheets can help you itemize, anticipate, and plan for both your income and your expenses. You can download free budget-tracking forms online or invest in a budgeting software or application, such as Quicken, Mint, or Quickbooks. Many of these tools connect to your bank account, credit cards, and even your student loans, making it easy to track your spending in real time. This can also help you to see how quickly things add up: a handful of $10 monthly subscriptions can cost you thousands over the course of a year!

> **Super official disclaimer!** We are creative artists and educators with a passion for advising, guiding, and empowering others. We are not certified accountants or financial planners. Information for taxes, contracts, unions, and so on is specific to your industry and region. We encourage you to ask questions and seek out the answers from qualified financial professionals.

We have budget worksheets at the end of this chapter to help you identify your personal and professional budget goals. Your financial goals and realities will change frequently, so you will need to update your budget as expenses fluctuate and as you move through the seasons of your career and life. Tax season can be a great time to update and evaluate your expenses, and assess what is working and which areas could use help.

Remember: this isn't personal, it's numbers. Getting comfortable with your budget is a step toward less anxiety around money and finances. Time to normalize talking about money!

Getting a J.O.B.

Entertainment is both a passion and a job. At different phases of your career, the passion can be more abundant than the job market, and getting a "day job" or "money job" is necessary.

We jokingly use the acronym J.O.B., which stands for Jumping Over Bills or Just Over Broke. Think of a J.O.B. as an opportunity for you to make money while you are gaining traction in your desired career path. When seeking employment that pays the bills, it is important to find J.O.B.s that are flexible, consistent, and, ideally, that offer opportunities to build your network.

Some people seek out a J.O.B. adjacent to their desired field. These can include teaching artistry or arts education, assisting an established professional in your field, and working for industry vendors or support services, all of which fulfill the networking aspect of a J.O.B. as you'll get to spend time around others who work in creative fields.

However, sometimes the best J.O.B. option is the one that is simply the most flexible, with the most consistent paycheck. Good options could be retail, data entry, online employment, substitute teaching, and service industry positions. Some creative professionals build a "companion career" that allows them to set their own hours as a personal trainer, accountant, notary, or consultant.

Do not feel shame or guilt for getting a J.O.B. Every freelancer has a great story of the crazy side gig they had at some point in their career. This is not a reflection of your success or lack of success in your career. It is a strategy to navigate a complex and ever-changing industry.

> **Camille's J.O.B.s:** During one two-year period, I worked as a children's DJ, a freelance fiction writer, made floral arrangements at a flower shop, wrote grants for a theater, and did search engine optimization and copywriting for a lingerie website. Each job

> gave me new skills and connections (and some great stories). One by one, they fell away as my creative career grew, although I continued to take occasional gig work for many years afterward! My J.O.B.s are still on my resume and shaped who I am as a creative professional.

Money Management: Expenses

Any career comes with expenses, both personal and professional. There are *fixed* expenses, which stay the same monthly or annually; examples are rent, car payments, health insurance, the average you spend on groceries, and monthly parking fees. You also have *variable* expenses, which include unexpected medical costs or car repairs, entertainment and discretionary spending (concerts, dining out, and theater tickets), gifts, and travel.

Many professionals, especially those who work primarily as independent contractors, choose to keep separate bank accounts for personal expenses and professional expenses. This system makes it easier to track reimbursable expenses and to do your taxes. For example, a costume designer who purchases an expensive international airplane ticket for a gig would run that expense through their professional account. When they receive a reimbursement a few weeks later, that would go into the same account, keeping large, temporary fluctuations from showing up on their personal account.

There are both fixed and variable expenses necessary for most creative careers. Website hosting, cell phone and internet bills, transportation, work clothing, union dues, membership expenses, and subscriptions are some of the most common work-related expenses shared by creative artists. Unions often charge a one-time application fee, a large initiation dues fee, and then annual dues that can be charged on a quarterly schedule. Memberships and subscriptions can be charged annually or monthly and may pay for themselves if you're actively using job boards or taking advantage of discounts. Plan for these expenses and be sure to consider whether the membership is still serving you before writing another check. You can save a portion of each paycheck for these expenses or deposit a few paychecks per year in anticipation.

You may have additional expenses related to your craft, like your kit, studio space, software, technology, and equipment. These are unavoidable, as you need them to do your best work. However, there are ways to decrease some of the larger expenses, such as sharing a studio space. If you are still in school or are connected to an alumni network, ask about whether your career or alumni center provides discounts on software or subscriptions.

Some expenses will be for getting your *next* job, like printing costs for your portfolio and resume, hiring a photographer for your work, and managing your website. Many creative artists include a "Marketing" line in their budget to track these necessary costs.

When it comes to professional expenses, imagine a triangle with a word at each point: Time, Money, and Labor. Any financial decision will usually involve choosing one or two and giving up at least one. For example, choosing to save money by doing something yourself, like making your own website, will often take more time and more labor. At a point in your career, it may make more sense to pay someone else to do that project, saving you time and labor. You will sometimes see this triangle as "Easy, Cheap, and Fast," meaning that something can be easy and fast, but won't be cheap – etc.!

Figure 8.1 Time, Money, Labor Triangle.

Source: Created by Jessica Champagne Hansen using resources from Freepik.com and Macrovector.

Taxes for Independent Contractors and Employees

Speaking of things that give you anxiety, let's talk taxes. They may be tedious and stressful but planning ahead can save your sanity – and your money! As we are decidedly not tax preparers, we will keep this section short and recommend you research best practices for filing taxes in your state, and for your area of employment. If you work in multiple states or live in one state and work in another, you may need to file in more than one state.

How you're paid for your gigs and jobs and how you claim that income is very important when it's time to file your taxes. The most common forms that you will complete when you start a new job in the United States are either a 1099 (for independent contractors) or a W4 (for employees).

A 1099 is for *independent contractors* receiving a payment above a certain threshold (usually above $600) during the tax year. If your income is filed as an independent contractor on a 1099, you will want to save at least 15% of your check in anticipation of that year's taxes, because it will not be automatically deducted or withheld from what you're paid. This means if you get a lump sum of $5,000 for a design gig, $750 of it should go straight into savings in preparation for tax season. Independent contractors are considered self-employed and may also need to pay business taxes for their city and/or state.

A Wage and Tax Statement form is for *employees* who have been hired by a company or organization on a full-time or part-time basis. When you are hired as an employee, you will complete a form that calculates the amount of money that will be withheld for taxes with every paycheck. This is an estimate; you may receive a check for a surplus after filing taxes or may need to contribute more if the estimate was not enough. However, someone paid on W2 is contributing toward their taxes automatically with every paycheck.

The differences between employees and independent contractors vary from state to state and can be confusing, for both workers and employers. Regardless of how you're paid, we recommend that you save a portion of your income each year in anticipation of taxes. Your first year as an independent contractor can come with tax "sticker shock," especially if you have not been setting aside a portion of your income in anticipation. As you grow your career, you will be able to predict and anticipate the trends for your taxes. We also recommend using an online tax calculator, which can help you plan for the year ahead with an estimate of your owed taxes.

Depending on the tax laws each year, how you're being paid, and the state you live and work in, there are job-related expenses that you can "deduct" from their taxable income. Deductions might include costs for equipment, studio rental, supplies, business insurance, home office costs, travel and working lunches, parking for gigs, theater tickets, and so on. You may also have special deductible expenses, such as childcare from a dependent savings account. It's important to keep all receipts and records, whether you throw them in a shoebox or scan them to a folder on your desktop. At the end of the year, you can ask your tax preparer which are deductible or sort through them yourself if you're doing your own taxes.

We highly recommend finding a specialized tax preparer who understands the entertainment industry and knows how deductions work for those in your field. This will save you time and money. Going to a larger, generalist tax preparation company could cost you more since many charge based on the volume of papers to process. If you freelance, this will add up quickly.

Contracts 101

In the simplest terms, a contract is a work agreement between you and your employer. Your contract outlines payment, scope of work, schedule, and responsibilities. A contract needs to be read, agreed upon, and signed, with copies of the fully-signed agreement shared with all parties, before you begin work.

In all industries, and regardless of your union status, you will need to negotiate and promote your interests for your contract. This can be an intimidating process. Some of us have a bad habit of skimming contracts or skipping to the signature bit. Break that habit now and review anything you sign, especially when there's money involved!

Scenery, Lighting, and Projection Designer François-Pierre Couture describes how he learned this the hard way:

> As a young scenic and lighting designer, I took on projects with small theater companies that seemed creatively promising. However, so much responsibility fell on my shoulders since small companies don't have the infrastructure of larger theaters. I often found myself compromising my ideas (or spending countless hours in the theater) just to try to make the production a success. I quickly learned the importance of reading contracts to fully understand the support I would get that would help me be successful as a designer. I did not sign anything that I did not understand, did

not agree with, or that would potentially jeopardize the product by putting too many responsibilities on my shoulders without production support.

If anything goes wrong during your project, you will be grateful to have this document. Often the language makes the information confusing and vague but seeks assistance to make sure you understand all of it.

If you are working as a nonunion independent contractor, you need to be prepared to draft and produce your own contracts. In fact, you have the right to do so! We asked Cheryl Rizzo, Managing Director for a mid-sized theater that works with both union and nonunion creatives, for her advice on how to create contracts as an early-career independent artist. She says,

> Start with a list of what things you know you need to make it possible to do the job. What is a reasonable fee? What equipment do you need to make your job possible? What time commitment are you able to give?

Think critically and try to be as comprehensive as possible; it is harder to come back after a contract has been created to ask for more time, money, or supplies.

Once you've made a list of all the basic details, it is time to organize them into a contract. Cheryl suggests, "find one of the million handy and helpful templates on the internet and tailor it to your style." The internet is a great source for contract research and resources. You can usually find examples of local contracts for your specialization online. Note that these can be fascinating, especially if payment amounts seem to vary from person to person, and are a great learning tool if you are early in your career!

Word of caution from Jess: Never, ever work without a contract. I once worked for an entire summer as a designer for a festival. I designed, constructed, fit, altered, and distressed two shows of costumes by myself (and with one hand in a cast from a comical rollerblading accident). After a full summer of work, there was never a paycheck . . . but there was never a contract, so there was nothing I could do. Without a contract there is no guarantee that you will be paid. Value your time and labor, and be sure to always have a contract *before* you begin work.

If you are a union member, your union will have a Collective Bargaining Agreement (CBA) with employers, which means you will use a Standard Design Agreement (SDA) as your contract document. We talked about the power of collective bargaining in Chapter 7, and the contract process is definitely an advantage of being a union member. CBAs have been created between unions and many different employers and industries. The union business representative office will have copies of all current, basic agreements for your review; these vary based on the local, region, and craft. All of them include a rate sheet with minimum pay rates, which are updated periodically as agreements change. Many industries, like theater and live entertainment, will have different groups and pay scales based on the size and income of the company. Even if you're not a union member, you can research the current union rate and contract agreement and base yours on this information.

> **NDAs: You just got hired for a big and exciting project with a world-famous company. You signed your contract and are getting ready for your first day. Time to go onto social media and share the juicy details of your amazing career leap, right?! No, not if you signed an NDA, or nondisclosure agreement, as a part of your contract. NDAs prevent you from sharing the details of a project publicly. Doing so could get you removed from the gig. Regardless of whether you sign an NDA, be very careful about what information you share and with whom.**

It is common for a freelancer to provide their own contract *and* to sign one provided by their employer. Cheryl says,

> Often managing directors and unions have their own contracts for working with independent contractors and you will likely need to sign that as well, but I am always impressed when I am working with an artist who comes in prepared with their own document. It means that I know the production is in good hands.

Don't be afraid to take control of a contract, instead of fearing it. It shows that you care about your work and are prepared and thoughtful. You can be in control of your contract even if you are not represented by a union.

Anatomy of a Contract

The format of contracts varies considerably by industry and position. However, there is consistency around the main components. Let's break it down.

The information in a contract usually includes:

- A cover sheet with basic information, sometimes formatted like a letter.
- Contact information and names for the employer and/or producer and the independent contractor.
- Details of the project, including a scope of work, deliverables (e.g. what is expected and on what schedule), and key collaborators.
- Salary or payment rate and outline of payment schedule, including whether payment is tied to specific deliverables or deadlines, as well as how the payment will be invoiced for and received.
- Information about what events or situations might lead to contract cancellation, and whether partial payment would be provided.
- Additional information about confidentiality, information access, safety, transportation, and/or ownership of work product.

This may be followed by one or more riders, which can include more information about the schedule of the project, deadlines, any travel involved, and special requests and accommodations. An example of an item that could be included in a rider is your housing and travel schedule when you are designing for a show away from your home base, with notes on what your employer is paying for. Don't be afraid to create a rider. It means that you are paying attention to all the details and clarifying the terms of your agreement.

Need more specifics? We asked François-Pierre to get granular about the parts of a standard contract, especially for nonunion work that does not fall under the CBA. We will look at fee, budget, scope, payment, and liability, which are all important parts of a contract.

Fee

Fee is what you are receiving for your work, whether it is as a designer, technician, consultant, stage manager, and so on. Entertainment industries with unions have minimum fees for certain types of work. If you are not in the union, you can still use these minimum fee rates as a guide.

François-Pierre reminds us, "Your fee should be competitive to what other designers at your level are being paid. It is okay to ask questions and ask for equitable pay!"

Budget

Next, consider the budget for the production or project. This is the money to execute the design. Be clear on exactly what is included in this amount, as sometimes the labor budget is also combined with the design or project materials budget. This can be shocking when you thought you had $8,000 dollars for costumes, but you actually only have $2,000 dollars after paying your costume production team.

If the fee and budget are combined, be wary. François-Pierre states,

> It is very important to ask for a fee that is independent of the production budget. Agreements like "the budget is $7000, and whatever you don't spend you can use as your fee" may seem interesting, but the problem is that everyone on the project wants the best show possible, yourself included. For an extra $1000 we could get a leather chair, or crown molding, and what if the director wants a different couch that would fit perfectly . . . before you know it, you are left with very little to pay for all your hard work!!

Scope

Scope refers to the extent of what you are being paid for, and what you are in charge of. This is critical and needs to be specific. If you are a stage manager, are you assuming you will have an assistant stage manager? If you are a lighting designer, will there be a head electrician throughout tech, or are you expected to fill in? François-Pierre explains,

> Many well-meaning companies assume that designers will not only design but will also build, paint, fix, maintain . . . Get ahead of this by being clear in your contract. What you are responsible for needs to be in writing to set clear boundaries. If you volunteer to help paint, etc. it must be understood that it goes beyond your initial contract.

Scope also includes the schedule details for the project. Be clear on your start and end date for the project, and how many hours you are expected to be present.

Payment

How and when will you be paid? The answer often depends on your industry. Television and film work is usually paid weekly. If you are an independent contractor in a different industry, you may be paid in one lump sum. In theater, you are usually paid in three installments, as François-Pierre describes:

> Usually, your fee is paid out as 1/3 upon signing, 1/3 at the approval of the designs, and 1/3 on opening night. Half at signing and half on opening is also used . . . but I prefer the first method since it leaves less money to be paid at the end.

Whatever the payment schedule is, be sure it is clearly listed in the contract.

Liability

Who is liable for injuries or accidents? It is crucial to address liability in a contract. François-Pierre highlights,

> Liability can be addressed in a clause 'holding you harmless' for any injuries, damages, or financial loss from your design. This is also another reason why I rarely build, rig, or do any type of structural work on my designs. I would rather let qualified (and insured!) professionals do the work and stick to design.

If you are doing work for which you could be held liable, be sure that you are aware of your insurance coverage through your employer or if you need to seek additional liability insurance as an independent contractor.

Intellectual Property

Do you own the rights to your designs or creations? The answer can be complex for creative industry workers. It can be very confusing to which extent you or the theater/producer/company you are working for are the rights holders of your work. A designer does have intellectual property rights over their drawings, designs, models, and conceptual models. Legally, no one can use your complete original design without credit and/or compensation. But what happens if someone rents 70% of your costume designs for their production of the same show and changes them slightly?

To help clear up this confusion, some designers use a special rider to address intellectual property rights. A common addition to this rider is the Right of First Refusal (ROFR), which states that you must be contacted first for subsequent productions of the same show before the offer can go to someone else. This will help you to protect your creative work and intellectual property.

Before you start drafting, do your research. Know what you need to make your professional budget, know what the industry rates are, and know what your expenses will be.

If you do decide to take on work at a lower rate, either as a favor or because you feel it is an exciting creative opportunity, you can take steps to ensure you aren't locked in to future work at that rate. François-Pierre shares, "To keep my hard-negotiated design fee rates consistent, I would ask if my contract could mention that this reduced rate does not reflect my normal fee and should not set a precedent for future productions." The more that you negotiate, the easier it will become!

Health Insurance

It's time for another Adulting 101 topic: health insurance. Your health and wellness are key to your career success and need to be considered in your budget. It can be tempting to forego health insurance to save money, but accidents happen and your health and safety enable you to continue to do what you love.

Health insurance is a large expense, but there are many options when it comes to coverage and plans. If health insurance is provided by your employer and/or union, money will be deducted from your paycheck each pay period to help cover your insurance costs. You can also get individual health insurance if you are a nonunion freelancer, or if your employer's plan doesn't have the coverage you want or need. Depending on your plan, you should still anticipate co-pays for appointments and medical bill expenses above your deductible level.

There are many options and you will need to do research and get rate quotes to choose the best plan for you. Just like taxes, information about health insurance changes each year and varies by location. Maintaining insurance coverage is mandatory in some states and strongly encouraged nationwide.

Retirement? Already?!

Do we really need to worry about retirement, especially if we just started working in the industry? YES! You should start thinking about your retirement plan on your first day of work. Setting aside even small amounts can be the difference between being able to plan for a rewarding retirement and feeling anxious about your future.

If you have been hired as a full-time employee, you are likely to have a retirement plan as one of your benefits; the most common option is a 401k, or retirement savings account. You can choose the amount to put into the 401k from every paycheck. Your employer will match your contributions up to a certain amount each year (read: free money! Hooray!).

If you are an independent contractor and freelancing or have one or more part-time jobs, you may have an option for a retirement plan in your union or you may need to start your retirement fund on your own. Each paycheck you receive, save a portion that you have determined for your retirement, even if it's a small amount at first. You will see the progress as you save over the years.

Setting an appointment with a financial planner can be helpful if you want to map out your financial goals for retirement and feel confident in your saving strategy. Some banks offer this service for free, and some even provide free classes on building retirement savings.

Time Management and Project Management

The creative process can be swift or lengthy, with projects ranging from a single day to many years in duration. Sometimes you'll be working on just one project, but often you'll be juggling two or three at once. In addition to your creative work, you have the administrative side of things to think about: emails, meetings, and other tasks. And on top of that, you have bills to pay, grocery shopping, a trip to the dentist, and yoga class. How do you manage it all and maintain the stamina required in the entertainment industry?

Time management and project management are crucial skillsets for creative industry workers, whether you are an independent designer or full-time administrative staff member. These are skills you'll hone over the course of your career. Some days you will be a time management boss and some days you'll feel like you're drowning. Having the following strategies in your back pocket can help you prioritize and get through the periods where you feel like everything is happening at once.

Start Big, Go Small
Particularly when you're beginning a new project, start by looking at the big picture. Any project has four main phases: ideation/brainstorming, planning, implementation/execution, and reflection/evaluation. Set goals and a timeline for each phase. If you tend to leap straight into the "doing" and miss deadlines, keeping an eye on big-picture goals and timelines can help you maintain focus.

Make Lists
It doesn't matter if you keep your task list on an app, a million sticky pads, a notebook, or in your email. Find a system that works for you and embrace the checklist. Lists let you visualize what you need to do in a day, week, or the duration of a project, and give you the satisfaction of crossing items out as you finish them! They can also help you set reasonable goals for what you can accomplish each day, especially if you include an estimated time for each item, whether it's five minutes or five hours. Organize your list the way it works best for you: by category, by project, type of task, or by the amount of brain power or creativity a task will take. Color-coding or highlighting can help you make a plan for which items to tackle first.

Chunk Out Your Calendar
Keep a planner and schedule your months, days, weeks, and even hours, especially if you're prone to procrastination. Start each day by reviewing what you've planned to accomplish, and then take some time at the end to look at the days ahead. Remember to block out preparation time before a major meeting, and to schedule in lunch and break time. You can also build your schedule around your most productive times. If you work best in the morning, block off two hours after breakfast for those projects that require serious concentration and brain power. If you like to finish work each day by 6 pm, block off that time and try to stick to it as much as you can.

Prioritize
One of the hardest parts of project management is prioritization, especially if you're juggling multiple jobs or projects. Look ahead at upcoming

deadlines or major project milestones and decide which tasks to tackle first. Is your list giant? Pick a few tasks that are not essential and put them at the top of next week's list. If you have a manager or boss, you can always ask for their help in setting priorities during a particularly busy time.

Evaluate

At the end of each week, month, and year, review what you've accomplished and evaluate how successful you've been. Are your systems working? Are you focusing too much on the small tasks and losing sight of the big picture? Look at what's coming up next: where do you see pressure points and moments where you can prioritize your health and wellness? If you're feeling stressed out or falling short of your goals, what can you say no to or remove from your task list?

Habits and Strategies between Gigs

If you're a freelancer or hold multiple part-time jobs, the natural ebb and flow of working in entertainment mean that you may find yourself with a few weeks or a few months between gigs. This gap may be the perfect time to employ self-care rituals and restorative practices. It can also be a moment for continued career and skill development.

> **A moment with Jessica the Organizer: Before working as a full-time professor, I often found myself with downtime in between costume gigs. This made me anxious as I have a bad habit of basing my worth on my productivity level. It can be motivating when I have a lot to do but difficult when there is a lull in my schedule. To balance productivity and rest, I came up with a strategy. I would start by giving myself a few days for relaxation, with no schedule or to-dos. The morning after my relaxation days I would make a plan and schedule to make the most of my remaining time between gigs, while still building in time to play and rest. I also tried to remember how much I would miss the relaxation time when I'm waking up for a 6 am call!**

Even during your time off, we recommend maintaining a consistent daily schedule. This will help keep you focused and will make going back to work a little easier when the break ends. Schedule time to check email, connect with industry contacts, look at job posts, and work on professional projects. Find a time to stop work-related activities each day and make sure you're allowing yourself plenty of time for rest.

To stay excited about your craft, focus on learning new skills that you haven't had the time to explore. Learn a new software, technical skill, or creative craft. This isn't just practical – it can help you reconnect to what you love about your work.

This time between projects is an opportunity to update your marketing materials and look for more work. You might update your resume, add photos to your website, and re-vamp your portfolio. Check job boards, but don't obsess. Schedule a time to browse them and then close them. Your day will be less stressful and more productive if you are not constantly checking for job postings.

Reach out to colleagues and friends and catch up with them. It is hard to connect with them when your schedule is busy and you never know when they might know about your next job opportunity.

Many creative people chose a career in entertainment, especially in freelancing, because of the flexible schedule and time in-between projects to take a break and play. Know yourself, your boundaries, your restorative practices, and your desire to learn new skills. This is YOUR time. Make the most of it!

Sustainability and Balance

If you just keep driving without stopping to refuel, you will end up with an empty tank. The danger of burnout is a reality of working in the entertainment industry. Active commitment to healthy boundaries, self-advocacy, and prioritizing rest and stillness are necessary to creating a sustainable creative career.

What do you need to incorporate into daily practice to feel balanced and fulfilled? Perhaps your ideal day includes a morning walk followed by a healthy breakfast, productive worktime, dinner with friends, and a full night's sleep. Keep those practices in your schedule, and then build in meetings, outlining a large project, checking in with your mentee, and updating your resume on your website. You won't have that "ideal day" every day, but practice prioritizing what makes you feel happy and whole. What you might view as the small things are key to fulfillment – and career success.

Because our work is often project-based, you may enter into weeks or months where rest falls by the wayside, and you have to look ahead to more balanced days. Sometimes it can feel like everything is happening at once: you accepted a huge new project and are going to be working longer days, the kids need to be picked up earlier from school and go to aftercare, and you're filling in for a team member who took another job. There may be nights when you're plugging away on the computer when it's finally quiet because everyone else is asleep.

During these busy periods, look ahead and block out time for rest and play. Perhaps you know that after this major project ends, you'll work on one small project Monday through Thursday in the mornings, spending the rest of your week on passion projects, playing with the kids, and catching up on sleep. Maybe you can block out a weekend getaway after a show opens. Just knowing that you have a vacation (or staycation!) coming your way can help you get through a particularly busy time.

No matter what your version of "balance" looks like, there are things that you can do on a regular basis to fill your creative tank and keep you from feeling burnout. Go to a museum, read a book, get good night's sleep, practice what you love, eat good food, take a walk, pet a cat, laugh with friends, watch a movie, listen to music, take deep breaths . . . these are the small things that we forget to do when we get too involved with work. In these small moments, you remember you are a human *being* and not a human *doing*.

Jess: Did someone say read a book? Reading is a restorative practice that reminds me how much I love art and creativity! Books about the creative process foster confidence and teach us how to be better collaborators. I recommend:

- *The Creative Habit: Learn it and Use it for Life* **by Twyla Tharp**
- *Big Magic: Creative Living Beyond Fear* **by Elizabeth Gilbert**
- *Creativity, Inc.* **by Ed Catmull**
- **Anything by Brené Brown, like, all of her books!**

Or anything you love! Reading is self-care.

What happens when we lose balance and burn out? Exhaustion and self-doubt set in, and your anxiety can stifle your creativity – making your seemingly endless amount of work even harder to tackle. If you start to feel these things, it's time to slow down. Time to connect with colleagues and friends, because we have all been there. Time to go back to your time management strategies and schedule in time for life.

And most of all, time to say …

No Thank You!

Let's practice saying one of the hardest words in the business: **No**.
Go ahead, try again, and mean it this time. **No**.
No thank you.
I can't participate, but thanks for thinking of me.
I won't be able to do it, but here are two colleagues who might be interested.
It's hard to turn down an opportunity. Sometimes the right answer for you at that time and for that opportunity is no. The reason could be scheduling conflicts, the time commitment, or just that you aren't excited about an opportunity. Practicing "no" is an important part of finding your balance and managing your time.

> **Camille <3s Boundaries:** My favorite shirt says "Boundaries are Self-Care." I was in my mid-thirties before I broke free from the guilt I associated with saying no or prioritizing play and rest. Now, I work hard to keep my weekends free of work responsibilities – and that includes seeing theater, as I consider that a part of my job! I also do my best not to over-explain my "no." If I decline an offer or say I can't participate in something, no one needs to know it's because I'm going to Monster Jam with my kids. Sometimes I don't have ANY reason to say no, aside from just . . . not wanting to do something. And guess what? That's as valid a reason as any.

Even seasoned professionals like François-Pierre struggle with saying no. He shares,

Saying no can be frightening, depressing, and seem like a failure. But it is empowering when done properly. It is better to be honest with a producer or a director and explain that the project seems very exciting, and you would really love to do it, but your current situation (whether it is financial, personal, or simply because you are too busy) does not allow you to do it but would love to work with them in the future. Maybe offer the name of someone you know and trust who could do it and follow up with them later: go see the production or just simply check-in. It shows that you are interested and keeps your name in their mind.

There are a lot of emotions that come with saying no but know that you can still stay engaged and in touch with the potential employer. A "no" doesn't mean the door is closed forever.

Remember that you are in control of your choices. If you start feeling like a martyr or that things will fall apart without you, that is a great sign that you need to set boundaries and consider stepping away. We care deeply about our careers and creative projects, but nothing is worth compromising your mental health or making you miserable. Sometimes "no" can set you free.

Figure 8.2 Budget Planning.

Source: Created by Jessica Champagne Hansen using resources from Freepik.com and Macrovector.

Budget Planning

Description

Budgets are a necessary task! This budget supports your financial empowerment by calculating your monthly expenses and income. If you have a combined or shared income, you will want to complete these forms with your partner. Does your income fluctuate month to month? Complete this form as an annual budget instead.

	Expenses	Cost		Expenses	Cost
Housing	Rent/Mortgage Electricity Gas Phone/Internet/Cable Water/Sewer Trash/Recycling Other:		Work Expenses	Website Union Dues Equipment & Software Publications & Research Supplies Other:	
Living Expenses	Car Payment Gas or Transportation Car Maintenance/Repair Groceries Household Goods Clothing Subscriptions Pet Care Personal Services & Care Other:		Debt	Loan Repayment Credit Cards Other:	
			Miscellaneous	Dining Out Entertainment Recreation Travel Gifts & Donations Savings & Investments Retirement Child Care Other:	
Insurance	Homeowner/Renter Auto Health Life Disability Other:		Total	Add up all of the costs for your expenses.	
Income					Total
Paychecks (total after deductions) Other:					
Total Income $ _____ - Total Expenses $ _____ = $ _____					

Follow Up

Once you've filled in the numbers, you'll have a clear picture about your budget and financial goals. Where can you cut costs? Where do you see potential savings? Highlight the areas where you think you can make a change and make a game plan. Look at you! You're financially empowered.

Figure 8.3 In-between Jobs Worksheet.

Source: Created by Jessica Champagne Hansen using resources from Freepik.com and Macrovector.

In Between Jobs Worksheet

Description

How do you spend your time between jobs? Find a balance between down time and taking time to focus on career related tasks.

Keep track of your daily tasks and habits for two weeks. Each day is numbered on the outside circle. Write your habits in each circle of the tracker and color in the corresponding box each day you make progress.

Sample

Daily Tasks and Habits

Job Seeking Tasks · Update job marketing materials · Learn a new skill · Networking · Other: · Other:

Figure 8.4 Your Week: A Pie Chart.

Source: Created by Jessica Champagne Hansen using resources from Freepik.com and Macrovector.

Your Week: A Pie Chart

Description

When you have a creative career, your days might look a little different from a typical 9 to 5 job. Sometimes, we get caught up in the constant to-do list and don't realize how much time we spend on each activity.

Look at the next page for a sample of this worksheet!

For a week, place a checkmark for each hour you spend doing tasks in the categories below when you are actively pursuing your career.

Emails	Doing my art	Other:
Meetings	Personal Tasks	Other:
Networking	Work Tasks	Other:

At the end of the week, add up your weekly totals from the areas above and list them in the Task Totals. Next, add them all up for your Total Weekly Hours. In the Percentage column, divide each task total by the total weekly hours. Example: 8 hours ÷ 40 hours = 20%
Color in the pie chart to represent the percentage of your time spent on each task.

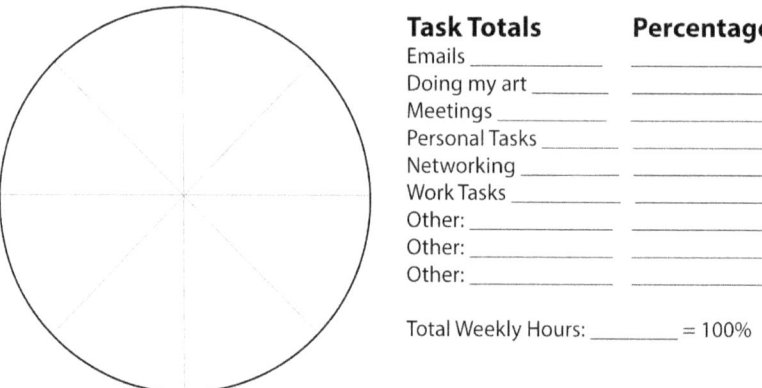

Task Totals   **Percentage**
Emails _____   _____
Doing my art _____   _____
Meetings _____   _____
Personal Tasks _____   _____
Networking _____   _____
Work Tasks _____   _____
Other: _____   _____
Other: _____   _____
Other: _____   _____

Total Weekly Hours: _____ = 100%

Follow Up

Time to reflect. Do you need more balance? You may want to look at the results and shift the way that you manage and spend your time. Make a game plan for the areas that don't serve you and work towards a better daily and weekly balance.

Creative Career Surviving and Thriving Skills ◆ 165

Figure 8.5 Your Week: A Pie Chart Sample Worksheet.

Source: Created by Jessica Champagne Hansen using resources from Freepik.com and Macrovector.

Your Week: A Pie Chart
Sample Worksheet

For a week, place a checkmark for each hour you spend doing tasks in the categories below when you are actively pursuing your career.

Emails
✓ ✓ ✓ ✓ ✓ ✓

Doing my art
✓ ✓ ✓ ✓ ✓ ✓ ✓

Other: Social media for work
✓ ✓

Meetings
✓ ✓ ✓ ✓

Personal Tasks
✓ ✓ ✓ ✓ ✓

Other: Update website
✓ ✓ ✓ ✓ ✓

Networking
✓ ✓ ✓

Work Tasks
✓ ✓ ✓ ✓ ✓ ✓

Other: Organize planner
✓ ✓

At the end of the week, add up your weekly totals from the areas above and list them in the Task Totals. Next, add them all up for your Total Weekly Hours. In the Percentage column, divide each task total by the total weekly hours. Example: 8 hours ÷ 40 hours = 20%
Color in the pie chart to represent the percentage of your time spent on each task.

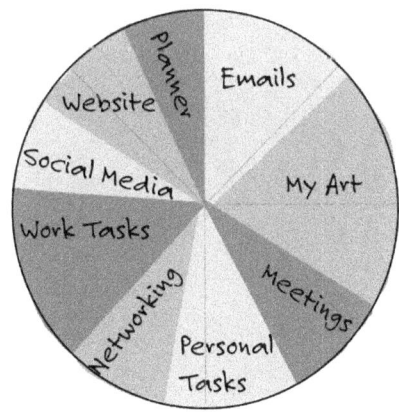

Task Totals	Percentage
Emails 6 hours	6/40 = 15%
Doing my art 7 hours	7/40 = 17.5%
Meetings 4 hours	4/40 = 10%
Personal Tasks 5 hours	5/40 = 12.5%
Networking 3 hours	3/40 = 7.5%
Work Tasks 6 hours	6/40 = 15%
Social media 2 hours	2/40 = 5%
Website 5 hours	5/40 = 12.5%
Planner 2 hours	2/40 = 5%

Total Weekly Hours: 40 hours = 100%

Follow Up — Time to reflect. Do you need more balance? You may want to look at the results and shift the way that you manage and spend your time. Make a game plan for the areas that don't serve you and work towards a better daily and weekly balance.

Part IV
Maintaining Flexibility and Finding Fulfillment in Your Career

9
Refocusing on Career Shifts and Wellness

Introduction

How many jobs will you have in your lifetime? What about distinct careers? Sources such as the U.S. Bureau of Labor Statistics, job-search websites such as Zippia, and independent researchers put the average number of jobs held by one person anywhere from 12 to 15 over their working life, across anywhere from three to seven different careers!

Sounds exhausting, to be honest.

Imagine, though, how this might play out for someone who studies stage management as an undergraduate. Let's call them Nico.

Nico graduates and wants to be a **theatrical stage manager**. They take on some stage management work and enjoy it, and begin building a network. They minored in technical theater and find themselves spending a lot of time with the production staff, especially the production managers.

When an assistant **production management** job opens at a theater they love, they take it. It's a great fit for their skillset, and they love the collaboration. Eventually, they move to another theater in the same city and lose the "assistant" part of their title.

Four years later, they get a call from a contact who's now at a theme park, asking them to apply for a **themed entertainment project manager** position. The money is great, and they accept the new challenge. They spend the next ten years traveling the world, working on a variety of challenging creative projects for three themed entertainment companies.

Eventually, though, they find out their college is looking for a new faculty member in their old department to teach stage management, production management, and technical direction. They can't stop thinking about it, apply, and get the position. Hello, **Professor** Nico!

In this scenario, Nico is around 40 years old and has had at least 7 jobs, across multiple industries and career paths! This is a common story for folks in entertainment, as our skills and interests translate well to a multitude of careers inside and outside of the arts.

In this chapter, we'll talk about navigating three distinct types of career shifts. The first is what we call a "pivot," where you change your role in industry, shifting from lighting tech to lighting design or from marketing to fundraising are examples of pivots. The next section will discuss coming into creative industries later in life, after a career elsewhere. We'll also talk about how your creative gifts and skills can be transferred to a variety of other industries.

It's our hope that everyone reading this book crafts a sustainable, healthy career, where they can thrive both at work and outside of it. The end of the chapter talks about wellness and how you know when it's time to rethink your work situation. In an industry where boundaries between play and work can get blurry, it's essential to set healthy boundaries and understand what brings you joy.

Company Man, from Camille: My paternal grandfather worked for the same company for his entire 50-year career. My mother spent more than 25 years working for the same school district, as a librarian, administrator, and classroom teacher. I'm going into my 11th year at the same nonprofit theater and hope to be there for years to come! I love the idea of creating a deep, rich, and lasting relationship with one organization or company, especially if it brings you continued joy and challenges. This kind of longevity is still possible but is less and less common. Are you a "company man" (or "company human!") or do you thrive on change?

Pivot!

One of the best things about diving into your career is being surprised by an emerging interest or passion. We complete our education with one idea about where our career might lead us; sometimes it's something we've studied extensively, or even wanted to do since childhood. Inevitably, though, we find our interests shifting as we begin to work. Often the shift is more about specialization or finding a "niche:" realizing you prefer designing for dance companies or that you want to put your technician skills to work in the cruise ship industry. What do you do, though, when you realize you are more interested in scenic design than stage management?

Making a "pivot" to another area of the creative industry requires self-advocacy and being clear – with yourself and others – about your aspirations. Here are some tips for making the shift (and taking your great reputation with you).

Identify Educational Needs and Find a Mentor

Think about whether you might need to invest in additional training to be qualified for a new gig. While this could mean a completely new Bachelor's or even Master's degree, often it could be as simple as taking one or two classes to fill in training gaps (often called "upskilling").

Sometimes you will be able to learn on the job, especially if the new interest is related to your existing profession. It's helpful to seek out a mentor who will talk to you about their job and support you in your pivot by bringing you into their professional circle. Perhaps this is the person who inspired you to make a change in the first place!

Note that you may have different pay rates for your old and new specializations, particularly at first. Sometimes, you may be taking union gigs for one area, and not the other. These dynamics can be tricky to navigate. Eventually, though, you will find a pay scale that works for all areas of your creative portfolio.

Multihyphenate or New Role?

Consider whether you are hoping to add this new area of interest to become a "multihyphenate" artist, or if you are looking at leaving your old role behind. For example, do you want to be a scenic designer/stage manager – a multihyphenate – or solely a scenic designer? This question can help you develop a strategy for making a change.

Being a multihyphenate is a beautiful way to build a portfolio career that allows you to explore many aspects of your creativity. It can also just mean more work (and more money) overall. Some multihyphenates are able to tap their full skillsets for some projects, acting as dual lighting and sound designers, directing shows they've written, or being both the designer and technician on smaller projects.

More and more creatives are embracing multihyphenate roles and finding ways to express the intersection of their talents. We asked Sean Cawelti, a true multihyphenate artist, about how he has navigated his career. From a young age, he was fascinated by puppets and telling stories with objects but often felt pressured to define himself using traditional terms like *director* or *designer*. He shared,

> My creative brain has always felt like a jumble of impulses and passions that never really made me feel comfortable declaring I am a singularity. This all made things like resume writing and website building incredible troublesome, as instead of one tab I needed several depending on the nature of the project. Even more irksome are the number of projects where I serve two roles such as Director and Video Designer or Video Designer and Puppet Designer.

For Sean, finding a term that felt right – Creative Director – helped him better articulate his multiplicity of interests. Creative Director, he says,

> Feels like home, along with terms like storyteller or just theater artist. I appreciate those terms as they help me to nest with ease the different passions and roles I take. I'm learning to embrace each project as a new opportunity to explore ways of creating and working, and that titles and roles shift wildly.

Finding a "niche" area that marries your skillsets can make you a major asset. As Sean says,

> Now I lean into the messy and embrace a duplicity of roles, not just for myself but encourage hop-scotching for others as well. The way I often learn to improve one aspect of my craft is by playing

in a totally different sandbox and borrowing slyly. The best art I've ever made has always been the work that defies simple categorization and I feel like that's true of people too.

Looking at building up new skills, while continuing to take gigs in your old focus area? You can consider a "sandbox transition" period where you continue doing your previous work while building a new portfolio, with the intention of letting go of your old gigs as the new ones ramp up.

Claim Your Space and Shout It Out
Remember: There is no official moment when an authority grants you permission to start calling yourself a designer, technician, stage manager, and so on. This goes for adding the multihyphenate "slash" to your current role. If you are ready to work in a new capacity, start referring to yourself in that capacity. Be open about the shift you're making and ask for people to consider you for opportunities.

In addition to updating your website, social media, and business cards to include the new area of work, reach out to current contacts and mentors with your news. If you're comfortable doing so, ask them to keep you in mind next time they're looking for someone with either of your skillsets.

Get Your NO Ready
There may come a time when you have to decline jobs in your old focus area in order to support your new interests. You may even reach a point where you remove your previous work from your resume, website, and so on, and you have to set clear boundaries for the kind of opportunities you want to pursue moving forward.

A pivot can be daunting, especially if you feel as though you've just established a reputation for yourself. The good news: it's easier to make this shift than it is to break into the field to begin with. It's also important to listen to that voice telling you to pursue your passion, even if it's inconvenient. Embrace your interests and follow your curiosity; those who love and support you will continue to follow you on your journey!

Entering the Creative Industries as a New Career

Whether you were a classroom teacher, served in the military, spent time at home with family members, or worked in a bank, the skills you built are welcome in the creative industries. Your unique background is an

asset. Never let anyone make you feel like you have to hide or downplay a previous career or life path.

You can decide how much of your previous work and life will come through in your career marketing materials. For example, you may create a section of your resume dedicated to this past career, or that acknowledges it with something like "10 years of experience in nonprofit fundraising" or "8-year Air Force veteran." Even if you don't describe every job in your previous career, referencing it in this way can help avoid the appearance of a resume gap.

We asked Sara Broadhead, Lighting Designer and Head Electrician, about her experience with a nontraditional career path. Sara told us she worked her way through college, first getting a business degree and working as an accountant. She says that accounting "Paid well, but was very boring. I missed the theater." She finished her theater degree over an additional four semesters and was eventually accepted into an elite Master's program for lighting design. After the death of a close family member early in her graduate program, she struggled to find a path for herself. Eventually, she embraced both her business and theater backgrounds and explored a variety of job options:

> I made a relationship with local theater and worked there over the summers as an electrician, programmer and designer. I also shadowed professionals in several areas of the entertainment industry. One day, I shadowed with a corporate design company. I graduated in June and started working there in September, and stayed for four years.

Now, Sara sees tremendous value in her combination of business and theater knowledge. She says,

> Graduate school taught me how to be a theatrical designer, and even a theatrical electrician, but my business degree set me up for doing estimates and proposals.
>
> While my position didn't require that I have the degrees that I have, they certainly have helped. I also believe that we learn something in every experience, positive or negative, that can be applied to our lives.

If you haven't already done so, take time to consider how your past experiences make you an asset in a creative workplace. Someone who has been a caregiver may bring patience, strategy, and organization to their new career. Someone switching from arts management to design may come with a deep understanding of the industry and knowledge of the financial and administrative sides of the artmaking process. It can be hard to outline these assets in a resume, but your cover letter is a great place to explain how your unique background makes you the best one for the position.

Being confident about your value will help you make a strong case for yourself as you enter this new chapter. You will walk into every job (and job interview!) understanding that the path you took made you into the artist and professional you are today.

Transferable Skills and Switching Industries

If you're considering a move outside of the creative industries – now or at any point down the road – we encourage you to look up "employability skills" or "what hiring managers look for." You'll find some version of the following list:

- Creativity
- Collaboration and Teamwork
- Critical Thinking
- Communication
- Time Management and Project Management

Now, look up "what the arts teach us" or "benefits of theater/arts education."

You will find *basically the same list*.

We are problem solvers. We love working in teams. We are creative, out-of-the-box thinkers who can still stick to a budget. We are planners, capable of breaking a project down into steps and meeting deadlines.

Some industries are particularly aligned with the skillsets gained through creative education. Many educators, lawyers, entrepreneurs, therapists, caregiving professionals, and people in public service positions have arts backgrounds. Of course, the entertainment industry is itself incredibly broad, with plenty of opportunities for career shifts as your interests and needs change.

Depending on what kind of career shift you're making, your biggest challenge may be communicating these transferrable skills to someone unfamiliar with your creative career. It's helpful to enlist a friend or family member from outside of the creative industry to make sure your resume and other marketing materials are scrubbed of insider jargon.

Brainstorm how you "translate" your skills to the new industry you're pursuing. Going into digital marketing from design? Think about how working with a director equates to working with a client, and how to use the language of digital marketing to describe your past projects. Moving from stage management to business management? Tweak your resume to focus on how a stage manager leads teams, organizes information, resolves interpersonal challenges, and maintains a high level of time and project management.

There are limitless possibilities for how to utilize a creative education in other industries. We'll share two of our favorite examples, from Congressional staffer Johnathan Garza and Rabbi Jessica Dell'Era. Both studied theater as undergraduates and see a clear trajectory from their arts background to their current roles.

Johnathan works for the U.S. House of Representatives and is currently on the Professional Staff of the House Committee on Natural Resources. He credits his theater education with his success and can identify a variety of hard skills he learned from the arts and applies daily in Congress. He shares,

> Both a stage manager and a Congressional staffer must be calm, organized, and prepared for any situation. Stage management taught me hard skills such as developing complex spreadsheets, tracking schedules and timelines, managing teams, and, just as important, managing the Director! All of these skills transferred directly to monitoring legislation, managing teams of staffers and keeping track of members' vote records.

Similarly, Jessica's dramaturgical background continues to support her work as a Rabbi. She says,

> I find myself drawing constantly on my theatrical upbringing, both onstage and backstage, as a religious leader. Some of the transferable skills are obvious, like public speaking for sermons,

singing for leading prayer, and memorization for chanting from the Torah. But others never occurred to me when I started out. As I began learning how to study Talmud, I found many of the thought processes and hermeneutic approaches felt inexplicably familiar. Why would I know how to do this already? I realized Talmud study felt a lot like table work for a Shakespeare production, parsing dense and canonical text for both minutiae and the larger narrative.

Jessica says she continues to be surprised by how her new career utilizes the skills she learned as a theater major.

As creative individuals, we may also be more attuned to emotion and empathy. Johnathan sees this in his work:

> Congress is an immensely emotional institution. Behind every policy change or decision is a story arc with a full cast of characters. There is drama between the lines of laws. Understanding the full story behind a particular policy and then dissecting character motivations allows me to make informed decisions. Also, it allows me to empathize with everyone, even when I don't agree with a policy decision.

Jessica agrees:

> Backstage work, particularly as a stage manager, taught me to read people and anticipate their needs, even those who didn't or couldn't ask. It also molded me into an empathetic listener. Through countless late-night tech rehearsals, which foster a natural sort of intimacy, I developed an intuition for when to offer practical advice and when simply to let the person express what was troubling them. Long before I decided to become a rabbi, cast- and crewmates were seeking me out when they just needed to talk. There's something about working together to tell stories, from all different kinds of perspectives, that teaches you how to hold space for others.

The emotional intelligence we gain from working in the arts is a superpower that can be useful in many professional situations.

Sustainability and Wellness

"Do what you love, and you'll never work a day in your life." It sounds so nice. It's too bad it isn't true.

Working in the arts has a tendency to take over your life. This is particularly true for those of us who have been conditioned to think that grueling schedules, no work/life balance, and an expectation of poverty and volunteerism are requirements for building a career in the creative sector.

Thankfully, year by year, we are pushing back against this harmful and unsustainable narrative. People, unions, and organizations are asking how we can shift our processes to promote safety and wellness.

When you look at your current job or desired job, think about the life you want to lead *outside of your work*, and whether this opportunity supports you as a whole individual.

You – yes, you reading this – deserve a career, and a life, rich with joy, rest, connection, financial security, and meaningful work. **This looks different for everyone.** Some people thrive in the excitement of gig work in the television and film industry. Some people enjoy the stability of a constant paycheck, while others prefer the flexibility of freelance work. Your needs and preferences are neither a reflection of your artistic capacity nor your ability to find a sustainable job in the arts.

It is also important to note that priorities change as you move through your life. The job and lifestyle you lead at age 25 may no longer fit your priorities in your 30s. Major life events, from the birth of a child to a cross-country move, may shift your approach to your career planning. Give yourself the grace to change your mind. Building a career necessitates a constant process of self-discovery, where we must look for moments of clarity around what brings us joy and fulfillment.

Support Teams

No creative worker is an island; we all need our support teams around us, whether we have a question about a contract or just need to vent. We've talked about mentors, networking, unions, and support around taxes and financial literacy. Let's talk about other potential members of your personal support team.

Agents and Managers

While many people associate an agent or manager with performing careers, those on the production and technical side may also pursue representation. This is usually a mid-career move, when your career has ramped up and you feel like you need support around managing the business aspects.

Agents and managers play similar roles in your career, but with key differences. Managers give career advice, work with you on your brand and portfolio presentation, and help you with career strategies. They may also help you find employment possibilities. Agents, on the other hand, focus on finding opportunities for employment and represent you during negotiations, including contract and rate negotiations.

As a freelancer, having this support system can take some pressure off so that you can focus on your work while someone else handles your contracts and negotiations. Many freelancers find that their bank accounts increase with this added support. Also, your network grows exponentially with representation, since agents and managers are in the business of knowing people!

A drawback, of course, is that this support comes at a cost and a portion of your earnings will go to your agent or manager. Note, though, that these professionals should *never* ask you to pay for anything *except* for an agreed-upon percentage of what you earn. Legitimate agents and managers will never ask you for fees up-front, or pressure you to take classes, or pay for additional services. Look up the laws regarding the fees an agent or manager can take in your state and be wary of anyone who asks for money outside of a portion of your earnings.

Finding an agent or manager can be a difficult process. Ask your professional network for agent and manager recommendations, research your local area, and check out the websites and portfolios of your colleagues to see who their managers or agents are. The working relationship with an agent or manager is important, so be sure to find the best match for you, your industry, and your work.

Affinity Spaces and Groups

An affinity space or group is a private community where all participants share a specific identity. Examples could be a group for LGBTQ+-identified staff members at a company, a community group for parents working in theater, or an affinity space for BIPOC-identified artists. Affinity spaces allow you to connect with others in a confidential, supportive environment.

Participating in an affinity space can be liberating. These spaces often serve dual purposes: they provide a confidential forum for connecting around all sorts of topics, and they often lead to collective organizing efforts to ask for changes that would benefit the group as a whole.

Friends Outside the Arts

People have friends … outside the arts?! Yes. It's true. While it can be wonderful "talking shop" about your career, maintaining friendships and relationships with people outside of your professional bubble can do wonders for your health and happiness. Sometimes a fresh perspective is just the reset you need.

Career Coaches

If you're feeling stuck or could just use an outside perspective, a career coach can be a fantastic investment. Career coaches spend anywhere from a single hour to many sessions with their clients, helping them navigate their career goals and even working with them on job applications or a game plan for career advancement.

Counselors and Therapists

A therapist or counselor can also be an invaluable member of your support team. Investing time in your mental health is crucial, particularly for creative individuals who may spend more time tapping into emotionally vulnerable areas. If you've never sought help in this area before, it may seem daunting. Remember you are not alone, and therapy is an effective tool used by millions of people on a daily basis. Therapy and counseling, like career coaching, can involve a single session or weekly appointments; your mental health professional will help you map out a plan to best support your needs.

What If I'm Not Sure What I Want?

Big and small career shifts are a part of life. Your interests evolve, your financial needs may shift, and new opportunities will present themselves. Whether you're thinking about entering the creative field or stepping outside of it, give yourself permission to pursue what feels right.

But what if you're not sure what "feels right?" Making a change can be terrifying, particularly if you're also looking at changes to your income, lifestyle, or location, and if that can impact your family or loved ones.

We asked an expert, Career Clarity Coach Serena Johnson, for her thoughts on how you know when it's time to go. Serena founded Get Me Out of This Job in 2018 to help people make much-needed career shifts, after working in theater for several years. She says,

> I always ask my clients what their priorities at this moment are. Is it to increase your finances? Is it wanting to try something new? Is it to find a role that isn't so demanding of your time? What do you need for you to thrive in life? How can your career support your life?

Once you do this deep thinking, it's decision time. Serena shares,

> Once you have identified your top priorities, you can see your next steps much more clearly. From there, you can then weigh your prospective career choices against these priorities. Does your current career check those boxes for you? If not, you know it is time to move on.

Whatever you decide, remember: **your background is an asset.** We are so much more than what jobs we have held or where we went to school. Every experience, every twist in our career journey only strengthens our self-knowledge and what we bring to our work.

In Chapter 10, you'll reflect on your next steps and create short-term and long-term goals. Remember that these goals may take you away from the path you – or perhaps your parents, professors, or friends – imagined for yourself. Change is healthy and sometimes you won't see the next phase of your journey until you've completed the last one.

182 ◆ Maintaining Flexibility and Finding Fulfillment in Your Career

Figure 9.1 Pivot, Shift, Refocus.

Source: Created by Jessica Champagne Hansen using resources from Freepik.com and Macrovector.

Pivot, Shift, Refocus

Description

At some point in your career, you may need to pivot, shift, or refocus. This is not a sign of failure, but of growth. Look into each of these scenarios when you're feeling stuck or craving some change.

Pivot

Making a pivot to another area of the creative industries requires self-advocacy and being clear about your aspirations.

Answer these prompts...

WHAT I NEED

WHAT CHANGES I NEED

WHO CAN HELP

Shift

If you're considering a job outside of the creative industry, focus on what will serve you in your new career.

List your....

SKILLS

NEW GOALS

EXPERIENCES

Refocus

Sometimes you may feel stuck in a career rut, in need of refocusing. Uncover the reasons you feel stuck, make some changes, and refocus your career.

Answer these prompts...

WHERE I AM STUCK

WHY I AM STUCK

HOW I CAN REFOCUS

Follow Up

Dedicating your entire career to one job, one industry or one field could limit your potential. Embrace the natural trajectory of your path and revisit this worksheet when you feel stuck at a crossroads.

10
Self-Reflection and Goal Setting

Time to Celebrate and Dream

There are patterns and seasons in our career, but sometimes we need to step back to see them clearly, learn from them, and plan our next steps. How did you get where you are? What did you learn? Whom did you meet along the way? How have you changed as an artist? What do you hope to accomplish next?

Creatives are dreamers, and we want you to take the time to dream big as you come to the end of this book. With seemingly endless uphill climbs in your career, it is important to reflect on your journey, celebrate your accomplishments, and set goals for the future.

In our industry, there is a natural cycle to our work. Theater shows, films, television shows, and trade shows all come to an end. When one project finishes, we move on to the next. This is true for everyone in the industry, regardless of whether you're a freelancer or a full-time employee. We're project-based people. These transitional moments can be the perfect time to pause, reflect, and set goals.

In the last nine chapters, you have investigated different aspects of creative career navigation. Using worksheets, you have created plans to support your personal, individual career exploration. Now, it's time to synthesize the work you've done into a Personal Career Manifesto. Don't worry, we will guide you through!

Celebrate Your Accomplishments

Your successes, both big and small, deserve to be recognized! Some of us are very good at celebrating our achievements, and others (including your authors!) struggle to give ourselves permission to honor what we've accomplished.

It may feel self-serving to celebrate each time you complete a drafting or land your next gig, but every day you are investing your time, energy, and talent in someone else's stories. Celebrating *your* story and *your* accomplishments helps you to zoom out to the big picture, appreciating how each little step you took along the way led to this moment.

In a world where we live a portion of our lives virtually, sharing your accomplishments online and on social media means your network can like, share, and applaud you. Did you reach a huge benchmark in your career? Share your big news with your network through email. Proud of your latest passion project? Post it with pride.

However, your accomplishment shouldn't just be shared on newsfeeds and in emails. Record your successes in your resume, CV, website, and other marketing materials. Each achievement builds upon the other and becomes a part of your career story.

By celebrating your accomplishments, you are giving yourself a moment to prepare for your next adventure and ensure you are ready to move on. This process of closure is essential, allowing you to look ahead to the next challenge. Remember, employers often look for emotional readiness, like empathy, problem-solving, communication, and collaboration, as vital soft skills in the people they employ. Be mindful of how you are feeling, both mentally and physically, before you go into a new room.

Your next gig or project will require as much attention, creativity, collaboration, and talent as the last, so take a moment to close the chapter on the last one, and look ahead with renewed spirit and joy.

Tools for Looking Ahead

As you move toward creating your Personal Career Manifesto, we want to introduce two helpful frameworks: growth mindset and emotional readiness.

The first, developed by Carol Dweck and outlined in *Mindset: The New Psychology of Success*, lays out the difference between a *fixed* mindset and a *growth* mindset. Cultivating growth mindset helps us see knowledge gaps as opportunities, and not failures. A designer in a fixed mindset might be intimidated by a CAD program and insist on continuing to hand-draw designs, telling others they're not interested in learning something new when their skillset is good enough. Conversely, someone leaning into growth mindset might continue to hand draft while also beginning to learn CAD. They would recognize that not being perfect at CAD doesn't mean they're a terrible scenic designer; it means they're learning. In short, we need to be vulnerable, open to new experiences and failures, and know that it is impossible to be amazing at everything.

Not amazing at everything?! Aren't we trying to be competitive in a fast-paced cutting-edge industry based on word-of-mouth job openings? How do we stay competitive, while also open to learning and vulnerability?

Enter *emotional readiness*, a companion to growth mindset, which can give us strong roots but flexible branches.

Emotional readiness comes down to self-knowledge and the ability to identify our strengths and weaknesses, without placing value on them. Understanding where we are strong and where we have room for growth helps us set learning goals. Cultivating emotional readiness prepares us for the challenges in our work and fosters healthy vulnerability, confidence, tenacity, curiosity, resilience, and more!

Psychologist and Professor Dr. Arpi Festekjian sheds some light on how we, as artists, can harness growth mindset and emotional readiness to build on our career success. She shares,

> You can display emotional readiness and growth mindset at the same time by being aware of your strengths, while still believing that there is opportunity for growth. As a person and artist, you have acquired many skills over the years that are available in your personal toolkit. Whenever you approach a challenge or encounter a new situation, use the tools you have available from past experiences and build on them by being open to learning. Embrace your strengths and perceive your areas of opportunity (we will not call them weaknesses!) as just that- opportunities for growth and change.

Arpi encourages cultivating a growth mindset by steering away from binary statements. Binary statements position you as *either* one thing *or* another, limiting your possibilities and categorizing you in unhealthy ways. Here are some examples of binary statements:

- I'm good at/I'm not good at...
- I'm the kind of person who.../ I'm not the kind of person who...
- I am not talented at...

Arpi notes,

> These binary explanations encourage a fixed mindset, one that does not appreciate the value of experience or practice. Even if it sounds positive (e.g., 'I'm naturally artistic'), you will take fewer risks because unknown circumstances or unsuccessful experiences in that domain may be a threat to your identity.

Having a fixed mindset limits our ability to see our own potential by pigeonholing us into strict categories.

How do we change the narrative to allow ourselves the freedom to grow? Arpi suggests, "By reframing your interpretations with effort and experience in mind, your approach will be a lot more hopeful and proactive, as you focus on what you can acquire with greater experience or knowledge." In other words, speak to what you know and what you have experience in, not what you *are*.

Here are examples of growth mindset statements:

- I can do ___ because I have a lot of experience.
- I cannot do ___ *yet* because I don't *yet* have the tools or experience.
- I may not have gotten that job *yet*, but this experience has brought me one step closer to my goal.

Embracing your potential for growth is essential in a competitive industry where you may hear a lot of "no," especially when you're first starting out, and where it can be tempting to compare yourself to others. Avoid this trap, says Arpi:

> It can feel intimidating to be around professionals in the field who *seemingly* are more successful than you. Comparing yourself to others not only thwarts your motivation, but also your creativity.

Your creativity is your unique stamp on the world-embrace it and nurture it with your growth mindset. See each experience as a step closer to your future career. If you believe you are on a path toward learning and growing (growth mindset) as opposed to a path toward winning and proving (fixed mindset), your motivation and zest for learning will bring you one step closer to acquiring the skills you need to achieve your goal.

Walk your own path and remember that comparison is the enemy of joy.

In short, you are not defined by your failures *or* successes, because you learn and grow from every experience. As you set goals and reflect on your experience, approach them with a growth mindset focused on what could be, using statements that allow for your own personal and professional growth.

Revisiting: Chapter by Chapter

The reflection questions below build on the worksheets you've completed throughout the book and provide an opportunity for you to synthesize what you've learned, planned, and dreamed about over the last nine chapters. Capture your responses in writing or use the questions as prompts to talk with a colleague or friend. Some questions will be easier to answer, and some will take some soul-searching. Tracking your answers over time will help you identify the areas that need extra attention and the places that you are totally rocking!

For each chapter, we recommend flipping back to review any worksheets you've completed, as well as skimming headings and noting anything that particularly resonated with you. If you skipped any worksheets, now is a great time to complete them.

Chapter 1: Your Art

- ◆ What type of creative work makes you feel fulfilled?
- ◆ Do you feel that your current work is at the "heart of the art?" How could you shift focus or dive deeper?
- ◆ Reflect on your Artist Statement. Have your feelings or aspirations changed in the time since you've completed it? If so, how?

Chapter 2: Your Career Planning

- Are you working in the field that best supports your skills, lifestyle, and aspirations? If not, what changes could you make?
- Reflect on your Career Vision Board. What changes would you like to make? Does it still feel authentic and exciting?

Chapter 3: Your Training

- What training or education has been most helpful to you, and why?
- What are you really good at? What comes easily to you?
- What are you still working on? What has been particularly challenging?
- What training or education would you still like to pursue, and why?

Chapter 4: Your Network and the Job You Want

- Whom have you met recently, and how have they (or how could they) impact your career?
- What could you do to build and maintain your network?
- Revisit the Networking Through Curiosity Worksheet. What are your new discoveries or areas of interest?
- Reflect on the Job Profile Worksheet. What excites you, and what are you looking forward to as you seek out future jobs?

Chapter 5: Your Marketing Materials

- Review your notes on your personal brand and aesthetic. Do the marketing materials you've created reflect these?
- Review your latest resume. What recent projects need to be included or updated?
- What additional marketing materials do you need to create, and what do you need to make this happen? (Examples: a weekend day to focus on it, money to set up a website, etc.)

Chapter 6: Your Interview and Negotiation Skills

- If you've participated in an interview, reflect on it. What went well? What could have been better?
- What are your personal "deal breakers" in a job?
- How prepared do you feel to negotiate? If you aren't fully prepared, how can you practice or feel more confident in your negotiation skills?

Chapter 7: Your Creative Community

- Have you found a community where you feel supported? If yes, where is it and how are you engaging? If no, how might you find a community for support?
- Is there a group or organization you can join, or a conference you can attend, that would support you in your professional growth?
- Revisit the Union or Non-Union? Worksheet. Are your answers the same or has your work shifted?

Chapter 8: Your Financial Empowerment and Thriving Skills

- What is going well and what is more challenging in your personal budgeting? Regarding the challenges, what steps could you take to feel more comfortable and empowered?
- What questions remain about financial empowerment, taxes, insurance, or other topics covered in this chapter? What professionals might you approach for support?
- Revisit the Professional and Personal Budget Planning Worksheet. What areas make you nervous, and what areas do you have confidence in? How do you build confidence around personal finance?
- Revisit the worksheet with Your Week: A Pie Chart Worksheet. How do you feel about the balance in your life, and the way you spend your time? What changes could you make?

Chapter 9: Your Career Navigation and Reflection

- What advice do you wish you had when you first began in this industry that you often reflect on now?
- When you began your career or your education, how did you define success? How do you define success now and how will you know when you've achieved your goals?
- Do you give yourself permission to change your goals as you grow and discover new opportunities and interests?

You have taken a deep dive into reflection on your career and celebrated your accomplishments. Now, we are going to create a comprehensive plan for your career journey, an accumulation of everything that we have explored together.

Creating Your Plan or Manifesto: Setting Goals for Your Future

In Chapter 1, you created an Artist Statement. You can think of that as your "why." You're about to create your "how." These Personal Career Manifesto worksheets will guide you through a process of goal-setting, designed to map out your next steps.

Let's break it down into six-month, one-year, and five-year goals. Examples of shorter-term goals may be learning new software, getting an internship, or scoring a gig. A longer-term goal may be branching into a new industry or writing a book (authors' note: nailed it!). Pace yourself and be mindful of all the steps involved in your goals. Ideally, your completed plan feels ambitious but attainable.

Regardless of whether you're setting short-term or long-term goals, it's essential that they are SMART. SMART is an acronym that helps you ensure your goals are **specific, measurable, attainable, relevant, and time-bound.**

- Specific: What is the goal, specifically? What are the exact steps to accomplish this goal?
- Measurable: How will you know that you have succeeded in your goal? What does achievement look like to you? How do you measure success?

- ◆ Attainable: Is this goal reachable in the time frame you've set, and given your resources, abilities, and commitments?
- ◆ Relevant: Does this goal support your larger career pathway? Is it moving you forward, in the direction you want to go?
- ◆ Timebound: How long will it take to achieve this goal, specifically? Are there internal milestones?

Figure 10.1 SMART Goal.

Source: Created by Jessica Champagne Hansen using resources from Freepik.com and Macrovector.

Specific
Measurable
Attainable
Relevant
Timebound

Clarity and specificity are essential. If you want to widen your network, your SMART goal could be to attend a conference with an emerging artist mixer and interesting workshops in the next three months. If you want to create more cohesive marketing materials, your goal could be to create a brand and logo for your website, resume, cover letter, and social media, completed within a semester.

Identifying the steps involved and setting smaller deadlines or milestones will keep you on track. For a six-month goal, this could be a simple checklist. For a one-year goal, it could mean calendaring internal deadlines to keep you on track. For long-term goals, you can consider creating a vision board for inspiration and goal-setting.

We have three different formats for mapping out your dream plans. You will explore a mind map, project overview, and a project tracker. Pay attention to which format works best for you and make it a part of your future planning rituals!

Your next (and last) step is to complete the career plan worksheets, creating your Personal Career Manifesto.

Goodbye, For Now!

You made it to the end, but really you are just beginning. There is so much for you to learn, achieve, and create.

This book, particularly the worksheets it contains, is meant to be a companion during your career journey. Use it as a reference book when you're prepping for an interview, or considering whether to join a union. As you navigate the new seasons of your career, revisit the worksheets with a fresh perspective to grow and plan.

Your network and mentors are there to support ambitious goals. When your aspirations feel unreachable, connect with them, and they'll remind why you set your goals in the first place. Progress is contagious, so surround yourself with fellow goal-setters, striving to be their best. Together, you will be unstoppable!

Our final advice for you is to pursue your career with a constant focus on exploration, creativity, and self-advocacy. You are the present and the future of the entertainment industry. It is showtime for *your* stories, and we cannot wait to celebrate all that you accomplish!

Dream big. Make a plan. Cultivate a network. Ask for what you want. And thrive.

Self-Reflection and Goal Setting ◆ 193

Figure 10.2 Personal Career Manifesto: Six-Month Plan.

Source: Created by Jessica Champagne Hansen using resources from Freepik.com and Macrovector.

Personal Career Manifesto
Six-Month Plan

Description: Part I of your Personal Career Manifesto looks at the next six months. Think of four short-term goals you'd like to set for yourself. Consider the steps to get from goal to achievement. As you finish each step, color in the boxes for the time it took you, keeping track of your progress.

Goal Description & Steps		Month 1	Month 2	Month 3	Month 4	Month 5	Month 6
Goal — Example: Learn CAD Program	Buy Software						
	Take online class						
	Receive Certificate						
Goal #1							
Goal #2							
Goal #3							
Goal #4							

Follow Up: At the end of six months, reflect on all you have achieved on the way to your goals. What was easy and what was challenging? What happened quickly and what took more time? Consider more short-term goals. It's time to plan the next six months!

Figure 10.3 Personal Career Manifesto: One-Year Plan.

Source: Created by Jessica Champagne Hansen using resources from Freepik.com and Macrovector.

Description: Part II of your Personal Career Manifesto looks at brainstorming your midterm goals. At the center of this mind map, imagine where you'd like to be a year from now. Write four goals in the outer circles and the steps to get there in the larger circles. Consider when you will work on them over the course of the next 12 months.

Follow Up: Now, take the tasks from each month and write them on your to-do list, schedule, or calendar. At the end of the year, celebrate your accomplishments and reflect on your progress. Carry any unfinished projects on to your next one-year plan!

Figure 10.4 Personal Career Manifesto: Five-Year Plan.

Source: Created by Jessica Champagne Hansen using resources from Freepik.com and Macrovector.

Personal Career Manifesto
Five-Year Plan

Description

Part III of the Personal Career Manifesto is all about dreaming big. This is as much about defining what you don't want as what you do want. Revisit the "Chapter by Chapter" section of Chapter 10 for helpful reflection question prompts.

Imagine 5 years in the future. Where do you see yourself in these areas?

My job	My next big career move	My education & training
My reputation in the field	My website/resume/experiences	My creative practice
My rest and joy	My family/friends	My creative community

Follow Up

Did you just dust off this book to check in on your five-year plan? Many of your goals will have been achieved and many no longer align. Some achievements were faster than expected and others slower. No matter the results, you continued to move forward.

Now, dream about the *next* five years of your career journey.

Index

Note: Page numbers in *italics* denote figures.

advocacy 133–134
aesthetic branding 74–75, 76–77
agents 179
alumni groups 60–61
American Theatre magazine 133
apprenticeships 46–48
Association of Arts Administration Educators 58
audio interviews 105

Bellet, Ashley 134–135
BFA programs 40
binary statements 185–186
Bornt, Emily 135–136
boundaries setting 160–161, 173
branding: aesthetic brand 74–75, 76–77; personal brand 74–76
Broadhead, Sara 174
Bruin, Brent 85, 89
budgeting 142–144, 152, *162*
business cards 65–66

calendar/planner 156
career coaches 180
career curation 57
career entry points 11
career guidebook overview 5–6
career guidebook worksheets 11–12, 190–191; Artist Statement *13*, 190; Budget Planning *162*; Career Vision Board *31*; Cover Letter Sample *90*; Education Priorities *51*; In-between Jobs Worksheet *163*; Job Profile *72*; My Creative Why *14*; Networking through Curiosity *71*; Personal Career Manifesto: Five-Year Plan *195*; Personal Career Manifesto: One-Year Plan *194*; Personal Career Manifesto: Six-Month Plan *193*; Pivot, Shift, Refocus *182*; Portfolio Worksheet *101–102*; Resume Worksheet *99–100*; review 187–190; Union or Nonunion *137*; Your Week: A Pie Chart *164–165*
career marketing materials: branding in 74–77; cover letters 85–89; curriculum vitae 84–85; morality in 84; need for 73–74; portfolios *see* portfolios; resumes 77–84; social media 97; submission of 97–98; websites 95–96
career shifts and wellness 169–170; and affinity spaces and groups 179–180; and agents and managers 179; capacity reference 173; and career coaches 180; and counselors and therapists 180; creative industries, entering 173–175; decision making 180–181; educational needs identification and finding mentor 171; employability skills 175–177; and friendships 180; making "pivot" 171, 173; multihyphenate artist, becoming 171–173; setting boundaries 173; and support teams 178–180; sustainability maintenance 178
Career Technical Education (CTE) 37
Cawelti, Sean 172–173
certificates 44–45
Childs, Jane 45
choosing art career 7–8
Clark, Courtney 74–75, 77
Collective Bargaining Agreement (CBA) 124, 150
colleges 39–42
commissions 132
communities, for connecting with colleagues 136
community colleges 37–39
conferences and events 132
continuing education 131
contracts 148–150
corporate design 27–28
corporate environment 27–28
Corrillo, Corinne 16–17
cost, of education and training 48–50
counselors 180
Couture, François-Pierre 148–149, 151, 152, 153, 154, 160–161
cover letters 85–89; examples for 87–89; format of 85–86
creative community, benefits of 123

creative industry profiles 15, 29–30, 72; cruise ship careers 25–27; design firms and corporate design 27–28; education careers 28–29; freelance (or gig) work 15–17; television and film careers 20–22; theater careers 17–19; theme park careers 22–24; touring careers 24–25
creativity, explained 20–21
Crocker, Andy 103–104, 116
cruise ship careers 25–27
curriculum vitae 84–85

degree *see* education, degrees, and training
Dell'Era, Rabbi Jessica 176–177
design firms 27–28
Diaz, Ashley 24, 25
directories, of organizational members 131–132
Director's Guild of America 127
Durbin, Holly Poe 43–44
Dweck, Carol 184–185

education, degrees, and training: community colleges 37–39; continuing education 131; cost of 40, 48–50; educational choices 34–36; educational pathways 33–34; education priorities 50, *51*; graduate school 42–44; higher education 36–37; theater training 18–19; training and certificates 44–45; undergraduate programs 39–42; value of creative education 34–36; work-based professional training 46–48
Educational Theatre Association (EdTA) 131
education careers 28–29
emotional readiness 184–185
employment seeking 56; *see also* job searching
employment support, by unions 125
entrepreneurship 67–70
expenses management 145–146

fees 151–152
Festekjian, Arpi 185–187
film careers 20–22
financial aid 48–49
financial liberation 140
financial literacy vs. financial empowerment 140–142
fixed mindset 184–187
Free Application for Federal Student Aid (FAFSA) 49
freelance work 15–17, 127, 157–158, 179
Frias, Cristina 8; art in life, importance of 8; career sustainability 9–10; connection art and life 8; life's fulfillment in the art 9; lifestyle choice 10

Garza, Johnathan 176–177
gig employment 15–17
goals setting, for future 190–191
Goldstein, Jennifer 27
graduate school 42–44
Graebner, Dianne K. 56–57
group interviews 105
growth mindset 184–187

Hansen, Chris 20, 22
health insurance 154
higher education 36–37
Ho, Howard 68–69
hybrid career 29

Ims, Meghan 41
informational interviews 62–65
in-person interview 106
Instagram 66
intellectual property 153–154
intensive, short-term training program 45
International Alliance of Theatrical Stage Employees (IATSE) 126–127
internships 46–48, 49
interviews: accepting offer 118–119; dealbreakers 112–114; feedback 116–117; financial and other negotiations in 114–115; following up after 115–116; interview day 108; overview of 103–104; preparing for 106–108; questions and prompts of 109–111; reference checks 116; rejecting offer 117–118; self-advocacy in 112; types of 104–106; weakness and strengths in 111
Interview Worksheet *120*

Jackson, Aaron 25–27
Jaen, Rafael 94
J.O.B. 144–145
job boards 58, 131–132
job searching: basics 58–59; entrepreneurship 67–70; informational interviews 62–65; networking relationships 66–67; networking strategies 61–62; networks for 59–61; professional reputation 55; seeking employment 56; self-producing projects 67–70; specialists vs. generalists 56–57; traditional networking spaces 65–66
job titles 59
Johnson, Serena 181

Keifer, Weston 29
Kennedy Center American College Theater Festival (KCACTF) 65

Latino Theater Company, Play at Work program of 46–47
liability 153
LinkedIn 63, 66, 97, 107
listservs 60
lobbying 133–134
local awards 60

major employers 60
managers 179
McMills, Ann E. 17, 18–19
mentors 15, 171
MFA programs 42
Miller-McKeever, Meagan 60–61
mindsets 184–187
Montecalvo, JM 128, 129–130
multihyphenate artist 171–173
Muslar, Elena 140–141, 142

national arts job boards 58
Nedreberg, Merrianne 106–107, 108
networking, for job searching 59–61, *71*; relationships 66–67; strategies 61–62; traditional networking spaces 65–66
networking, organizational 132
nonunion life 127–129; benefits of 128; challenges of 128–129; worksheet *137*
"no" saying (turning down opportunity) 160–161

one-on-one interviews 105
one-way video interviews 105
online groups 135–136

panel interviews 105–106
payments 153
permanent projects 27
personal branding 74–76, *75–76*
personal career manifesto, frameworks for 184–187, 190–191, *193–195*
phone interviews 105
portfolios: digital (pdf) portfolios 91, 92; format of 89–91; labels 94; organizing 92–93; page layout 93–94; photos 94; physical book portfolios 91–92; updating and editing 94–95; worksheet for *101–102*
Prague Quadrennial of Performance and Design Space 132

professional networking sites 63, 66
professional organizations and groups: advocacy and lobbying 133–134; commissions and working groups 132; conferences and events 132; continuing education 131; job boards and directories 131–132; networking 132; publications 133; study tours 132
professional reputation 55
profiles *see* creative industry profiles
project management 155–156
publications 133

Ramirez, Sergio 34–36
reality of careers in entertainment 6–7
resumes: areas of interest 81; education overview 79; examples for 79–81; name and contact information in 79; references 83; skills 81–82; work experience overview 79–80; worksheet for *99–100*
retirement 155
Right of First Refusal (ROFR) 154
Rivera, Victoria Inez 37–38, 39
Rizzo, Cheryl 149, 150
role-play 107
Rucker, Ashleigh Akilah 29

scope, of payment and role 152
Scott, Angela 46–47
self-advocacy 112
self-doubt 47–48
self-knowledge 185
self-producing 67–70, *69–70*
self-reflection 183–187
Sightlines (USITT newsletter) 133
skillsets 139; boundaries setting 160–161; budgeting 142–144, 152; calendar/planner keeping 156; contracts 148–150; expenses management 145–146; fee 151–152; financial literacy vs. financial empowerment 140–142; habits and strategies between gigs 157–158, *163*; health insurance 154; intellectual property 153–154; J.O.B. 144–145; liability 153; lists preparation 156; new project phases 156; payment 153; resumes 77–78; retirement 155; scope 152; sustainability and balance 158–160; task list evaluation 156; task prioritization 156–157; taxes 146–148; time management and project management 155–156
SMART goals 190–191, *191*

social media: and job searching 60; presence in 97, 135–136, 184
Southeastern Theatre Conference (SETC) 132
specialists vs. generalists 56–57
specialty trainings 45
Standard Design Agreement (SDA) 150
Steadman, Josh 23
student loans 49
study tours 132
summer stock 18–19
superconnectors 66
support systems for creative careers 178–180
sustainability and balance 158–160

task list evaluation 156
task prioritization 156–157
taxes 146–148
TD&T (Theater Design & Technology) magazine 133
Teamsters 127
teamwork 23
television careers 20–22
temporary projects 27
theater careers 17–19
Theatre Communications Group (TCG) 133
Themed Entertainment Association (TEA) 131
theme park careers 22–24
therapists 180
Time, Money, and Labor triangle 146, *146*

time management 155–156
touring careers 24–25
training *see* education, degrees, and training

undergraduate programs 39–42
unions: benefits of 128; collective bargaining agreements 124; Director's Guild of America 127; and employment support 125; International Alliance of Theatrical Stage Employees (IATSE) 126–127; joining 129–130; membership in 126; and nonunion life 127–129; overview 124; Teamsters 127; worksheet *137*
United States Institute for Theatre Technology (USITT) 65, 133, 134–135
universities 39–42
University Resident Theatre Association (URTA) 44
upskilling 171

Veenstra, Joel 36–37
videoconference interviews 105
visual aesthetics 76–77

website resources 58
work-based professional training 46–48
working groups 132
workplace culture 112
World Stage Design 132
Wyenn, Diana 69

For Product Safety Concerns and Information please contact our EU
representative GPSR@taylorandfrancis.com
Taylor & Francis Verlag GmbH, Kaufingerstraße 24, 80331 München, Germany

www.ingramcontent.com/pod-product-compliance
Lightning Source LLC
Chambersburg PA
CBHW080410300426
44113CB00015B/2465